Bloom's

GUIDES

Amy Tan's
The Joy Luck Club

The Adventures of Huckleberry Finn

All the Pretty Horses

Animal Farm

The Autobiography of Malcolm X

The Awakening

The Bell Jar

Beloved

Beowulf

Black Boy

The Bluest Eye

Brave New World

The Canterbury Tales

Catch-22

The Catcher in the Rye

The Chosen

The Crucible

Cry, the Beloved Country

Death of a Salesman

Fahrenheit 451

A Farewell to Arms

Frankenstein

The Glass Menagerie

The Grapes of Wrath

Great Expectations

The Great Gatsby

Hamlet

The Handmaid's Tale

Heart of Darkness

The House on Mango Street

I Know Why the Caged Bird Sings

The Iliad

Invisible Man

Jane Eyre

The Joy Luck Club

The Kite Runner

Lord of the Flies

Macbeth

Maggie: A Girl of the Streets

The Member of the Wedding

The Metamorphosis

Native Son

Night

1984

The Odyssey

Oedipus Rex

Of Mice and Men

One Hundred Years of Solitude

Pride and Prejudice

Ragtime

A Raisin in the Sun

The Red Badge of Courage

Romeo and Juliet

The Scarlet Letter

A Separate Peace

Slaughterhouse-Five

Snow Falling on Cedars

The Stranger

A Streetcar Named Desire

The Sun Also Rises

A Tale of Two Cities

Their Eyes Were Watching God

The Things They Carried

To Kill a Mockingbird

Uncle Tom's Cabin

The Waste Land

Wuthering Heights

Bloom's
GUIDES

Amy Tan's
The Joy Luck Club

Edited & with an Introduction
by Harold Bloom

BLOOM'S
LITERARY CRITICISM
An imprint of Infobase Publishing

Bloom's Guides: The Joy Luck Club

Copyright © 2009 by Infobase Publishing

Introduction © 2009 by Harold Bloom

Bloom's Literary Criticism
An imprint of Infobase Publishing
132 West 31st Street
New York, NY 10001

Library of Congress Cataloging-in-Publication Data
Amy Tan's The Joy Luck Club / edited and with an introduction by Harold Bloom.
    p. cm. — (Bloom's guides)
    Includes bibliographical references and index.
    ISBN 978-1-60413-574-9
    1. Tan, Amy. Joy Luck Club. 2. Chinese Americans in literature.
    I. Bloom, Harold. II. Title. III. Series.
    PS3570.A48J6324 2010
    813'.54—dc22   2009016268

Contributing editor: Portia Williams Weiskel
Cover designed by Takeshi Takahashi
Printed in the United States of America
IBT IBT 10 9 8 7 6 5 4 3 2 1
This book is printed on acid-free paper.

Contents

Introduction

HAROLD BLOOM

In an accomplished essay, Myra Jehlen sees Amy Tan, against all odds, returning to Whitman's stance and singing a latter-day *Song of Myself*. That implicitly is high praise and, if justified, might give *The Joy Luck Club* an aesthetic dignity beyond the popular success it continues to enjoy. Will it be a permanent part of the revised canon of an American literature "opened up" by consideration of gender and ethnicity, or will it prove only another period piece, in which we currently abound?

Amy Tan is a skilled storyteller and a remarkable personality. Jehlen charmingly says: "Amy Tan has read her Emerson, and she doesn't believe him. This is not surprising, as he probably would have doubted her." I would murmur that it all depends upon *which* Emerson Tan has read, as there are so many. Having met and admired Tan, I would recommend *The Conduct of Life*, which is consonant with her rugged but amiable stance toward reality.

Jehlen eloquently concludes by stating both Tan's relation to Whitman and the significant differences:

> Jing-Mei becomes herself finally when, like Whitman, she can be the writer of the Body and the writer of the Soul, can sing both others and herself. If she is Whitman's critic as well as his descendant, it is because America has lost its innocence in the matter of individualism. Moreover, the duplicities of the notion of the universal self have been revealed in our time especially by the protestations of people of Amy Tan's kind: women and non-whites. It is not surprising that Jing-Mei's claim be not as universal as Whitman's, nor that its costs be apparent. It is surprising to find her claiming the old transcendent, appropriating self at all, and, in the name of culture, singing a latter-day "Song of Myself."

Jehlen is aware, as I am, that Whitman attempted to speak for women as for men and for all ethnic strains. What she doubts is the Whitmanian possibility of universal representation, since we are in a time of group identities: gendered, diversely oriented sexual preferences, ethnicities. And yet Whitman, at his best, permanently has reached and held a universal audience. *Song of Myself* is not a period piece.

Biographical Sketch

Turbulent lives generate memorable stories, and Amy Tan's predecessors provided her with abundant material for her novels. A suicide, a deformed child, and the "healing" of one relative by eating a small piece of the flesh of another all occurred in the generation of her great-grandparents.

Tan's maternal grandmother, Jing-mei, lost her scholar husband to influenza in 1924 and involuntarily became a "replacement wife" for one of the four wives in a household headed by a wealthy man. One critic familiar with Tan's ancestry (E.D. Huntley, *Amy Tan: A Critical Companion*) reports that Jing-mei was driven to suicide when a son she gave birth to was claimed by another wife. Whatever the circumstances, the suicide is an established fact. On New Year's Day in 1925, Tan's grandmother swallowed raw opium deliberately hidden in rice cakes and died in the presence of her nine-year-old daughter, Daisy (from the earlier marriage), who would become Amy Tan's mother. Mary Ellen Snodgrass reports (in *Amy Tan: A Literary Companion*) that Daisy later revealed the shame associated with parental suicide: "We had no face! We belonged to nobody!" (7).

In 1935, when Daisy was nineteen, relatives arranged a marriage for her with a pilot in the Kuomintang Air Force, a mate who proved to be distant and abusive. Daisy was still married to her pilot husband when she met John Yuehhan Tan, Amy Tan's father, on a riverboat journey in southwestern China. Four years later, in 1945, on a street in Tientsin, the two had an unexpected encounter and acknowledged their mutual attraction. In 1947, Daisy escaped from her husband (leaving behind three daughters) and was subsequently put on trial for adultery with John Tan and imprisoned for two years. In 1949, she immigrated to California to marry John, escaping, as it turned out, five days before the communist takeover closed the borders. It is this ancestral history that Amy Tan inherited.

When Tan was born—in 1952 in Oakland, California—she was given the Chinese name An-mei, which means "blessing from America." In an interview with *Cosmopolitan* magazine after the publication of *The Joy Luck Club*, Tan explained to interviewer Joan Chatfield-Taylor: "Immigrant parents come to America with the idea that they are going to lose ground, economically and socially, but that their children will eventually benefit from what they have done" (Snodgrass 8). The particular cluster of expectations implied in this observation and the emotional power animating them created the pervasive and persistent family and cultural conflicts that Amy Tan experienced in her own life and later featured in her widely acclaimed novels.

Success as an American-born child of immigrant parents required assimilating to a certain extent to American culture, a process that unavoidably involved some rejection of Chinese customs and assumptions dear to the hearts of immigrant parents and so necessary for their own psychological survival. A few details from Tan's earliest years are emblematic of this tension. At age ten, she clipped her nose with a clothespin at night to give it what she hoped would be a slimmer, more American-looking shape. She understood Mandarin but spoke only English. She found refuge from her mother's cautionary stories about menacing forces and doomed destinies by reading about life on the prairie in Laura Ingalls Wilder's books. She hated her obligatory piano lessons so much that when she later met child prodigy pianist Ginny Tiu (made popular by appearing on *The Ed Sullivan Show*) she told her that she had resented her as a child. Tan did not want her friends to come for dinner, fearing the humiliation that would ensue from their discovery that her mother served fish with its head still attached. Tan is quoted in a 1990 review of *The Joy Luck Club* as wishing she had a mother like the bland but never embarrassing one played by Jane Wyman in the 1950s television show *Father Knows Best*.

The suffering produced by trying to navigate the contradictions between her ethnic upbringing and the ubiquitous influences of American culture is likely responsible for the spells of anger and depression Tan experienced at a young age. Still a child of six years, she reacted to some

Cedarbrae 416-396-8850

Toronto Public Library

User ID: 2 ********* 9984

Date Format: DD/MM/YYYY

Number of Items: 4

Item ID:37131121318943
 Title:Amy Tan's The Joy Luck Club
 Date due:31/08/2015

Item ID:37131121285720
 Title:Daughters-in-law
 Date due:31/08/2015

Item ID:37131159877562
 Title:One pair of feet : the entertaining
memoirs of a young nurse during World
War II
 Date due:31/08/2015

Item ID:37131083894824
 Title:Amy Tan
 Date due:31/08/2015

Telephone Renewal# 416-395-5505
www.torontopubliclibrary.ca
 Monday, August 10, 2015   2:50 PM

unexpressed emotion by cutting her wrist with a butter knife. By her own admission—and as reported in some recent accounts of her life—periods of depression are an ongoing challenge for her. She summarized the struggles she and her brother Peter experienced during these years for a reporter for *The Los Angeles Times* (May 12, 1989): "[Our] parents wanted us to have American circumstances and Chinese character" (Huntley 2).

Despite these difficulties, Tan's childhood and youth featured many positive elements. She was close to her father, an engineer turned Baptist minister, who read aloud his sermons to her and entrusted her with making suggestions that would clarify and strengthen his Sunday morning teachings. She even had that most coveted and most all-American teenage job of the era—being a carhop or outdoor waitress at an A&W stand. Like the mothers in *The Joy Luck Club*, Tan's mother and friends regularly gathered at their home (like the "aunties") to tell stories, play mah jong games, and cook old-country recipes. Tan's childhood was enriched as well by her enthusiasm for reading. At the library she had access to books her parents might have forbidden or would not otherwise have known about, such as *The Catcher in the Rye* and *To Kill a Mockingbird*.

A double misfortune struck the family when, in 1967, sixteen-year-old Peter moved rapidly from depression into a fatal coma brought on by a tumor in his brain, and less than a year later, John Tan died, also from a malignant brain tumor. Mother and daughter were grief stricken, but Daisy reacted in a way that some judged to be recklessly irrational. In need of some explanation for these twin catastrophes, she turned against her recently acquired Christian faith and toward a superstitious fear that malicious forces inhabited the family home causing a curse to fall on the inhabitants. After disappointing experiences with "spirit guides" and the failure of feng shui practitioners to bring clarity or calm, Daisy fled with her daughter and other son, John, to Switzerland. This period coincided with Tan's most flagrant adolescent behaviors. Determined to rescue her daughter from a reckless and dangerous elopement, Daisy engaged in some discreet detective work that exposed the boyfriend's drug dealing and led to his arrest.

After completing high school in Switzerland, Tan returned to California to pursue a career in neurosurgery, her mother's longtime plan for her. Eventually she found her way to San Jose State University to be near her lawyer boyfriend and to double-major in linguistics and literature. These decisions precipitated a prolonged estrangement between Tan and her mother, a gulf that was exacerbated by Tan's decision in 1974 to marry the lawyer, an Italian American named Louis De Mattei.

The shocking murder of a friend and neighbor set Tan's life in yet another direction. Traumatized by the loss and having to testify as a witness in the subsequent trial, Tan was unable to stay in school. She began work with mentally disabled children and four years later became the director of a San Francisco agency doing similar work. In this capacity, she was spending her time with parents and children experiencing the shock that comes when disability is first diagnosed and then helping these families confront the related family issues that would later inform her own writing.

Tan was eight when she had her first publishing success; her third-grade essay "What the Library Means to Me" was printed in the *Santa Rosa Press Democrat* in 1960. Twenty-one years later, in 1981, she published journalism pieces called *Emergency Room Reports*, but for most of that decade she did business writing such as technical how-to documents and speeches for executives of communications companies. This kind of writing did not make her happy, but it made her financially secure and able to provide a sense of security for her mother.

Tan's interest in writing novels—in retrospect seemingly inevitable—was first triggered by her own reading of novels for stimulation and escape during childhood and strengthened by her realization of her mother's importance to her after Daisy's sudden hospitalization for symptoms of a heart attack. Daisy returned to health, but this reminder of her mother's mortality was transformative for the daughter. Tan could now stop rebelling long enough to see her mother objectively—as a real person with her own long-buried griefs and long-deferred hopes—and appreciate her for being a source of emotional and cultural insight and wisdom. Tan was at the time also in possession of the information revealed to her by Daisy after the deaths of her husband and son that, like the character June in her first novel, she had half-sisters living in China. Also like June, Tan traveled to China (in 1987), accompanied by her mother, to meet the sisters and to embrace the culture and country that was her legacy through her parents. Of this momentous experience, Tan wrote (see Ellen Kanner, *Bookpage*, December 1995, 3): "When you go to a country that's the home of your ancestors, there's more than the issue of birthplace, there's a geography that's in essence spiritual."

Within weeks of releasing *The Joy Luck Club* on March 22, 1989, Amy Tan was a national celebrity and soon thereafter a spokeswoman for ethnic and crosscultural issues. She was also caught in controversy; the wildly popular novel was praised for its compelling storytelling and for raising feminist issues in an ethnic setting, but it was criticized for being insufficiently political and for presenting American culture as "progressive" and Chinese culture as "backward." This controversy is ongoing. Tan continues to publish: *The Kitchen God's Wife* (1991); *The Moon Lady*, a children's book (1992); *The Chinese Siamese Cat*, a second children's book (1994); *The Hundred Secret Senses* and *The Year of No Flood* (1995); *The Bonesetter's Daughter* (2001); *The Opposite of Fate: A Book of Musings*, reflections on life (2003); and *Saving Fish from Drowning* (2005). For her work, Tan has been nominated for and received numerous literary prizes and recognitions. When Daisy died of Alzheimer's disease in 1999, Tan found herself feeling unexpectedly lonely and vulnerable. She had had the satisfaction of witnessing her mother's pleasure and pride in her daughter's successes and Daisy's profound gratitude for knowing that her own arduous and heart-wrenching experiences had finally been given voice and life in her daughter's novels.

Recently Tan's life has been compromised by the neurological, emotional, and physical impairments associated with Lyme disease, a condition not diagnosed accurately until 2001. Despite her condition, she has managed to stay active and engaged. She belongs to a literary band called the Rock Bottom Remainder and frequently sings her signature song, the Nancy Sinatra hit "These Boots Were Made for Walking." In 1996, on a fundraising trip to China, Tan encountered some diplomatic resistance, which resulted in an official ban on any further travel in the country. She has explicitly asserted her intention to refrain from making public commentary on Chinese politics, but she has continued to contribute to groups offering educational and medical services in China and Tibet. She also made a public protest against the American invasion of Iraq, joining fellow writers Wally Lamb and Stephen King in a full-page statement in *The New York Times* of March 20, 2003.

Tan continues to live with her husband in California and New York City. She has two dogs and one cat but chose not to have children. In 2001, she told a reporter for *USA Today*, "I was afraid that I would pass on a lot of the fears I grew up with" (February 19, pp. 1D–2D). The weight of one's personal history manifests itself differently for each person. Tan's creative energies have gone into creating memorable characters inhabiting compelling lives and who offer important insights to her readers.

The Story Behind the Story

The publication of *The Joy Luck Club* in 1989 gave rise to the author's near-instant fame, widely known as "the Amy Tan phenomenon." Originally meant to appear as a series of short stories, the novel form it finally took was the idea of Tan's agent and editors, who arranged the prepublication promotion as well. When G. P. Putnam & Sons released the first edition, words of high praise from Alice Walker, Louise Erdrich, and Alice Hoffman were prominently featured on the dust jacket.

In its first year of publication *The Joy Luck Club* was the longest-running hardcover (thirty-four weeks) on the *New York Times* bestseller list; its paperback edition stayed on the list for nine months. Within the year, the novel became a selection for the Quality Paperback Book Club and the Book-of-the-Month Club. It won the Commonwealth Club Gold Award and the Bay Area Book Reviewers' award for new fiction and was nominated for many other prestigious national literary awards. Other distinctions for the novel include twenty-seven hardcover reprintings and translation into more than two dozen languages.

A highly successful commercial adaptation of the novel into film was made by director Wayne Wang, who insisted that no non-Asian actors be given roles written for Asian characters. The time between the publication of the novel and the call for auditions for the film was sufficient to inspire nearly 400 women to read for one of the mother roles. According to those who interviewed these actresses, many of them told heart-wrenching personal stories to explain their interest in participating in the film. (Additional information about the making of the film can be found in Peter X. Feng's book on Asian-American film and video, *Identities in Motion*, 2002).

A success of this magnitude invites questions: Why is *The Joy Luck Club* so popular, and how are we to judge the nature and

15

implications of this popularity? Jane Elliott (in *Popular Feminist Fiction as American Allegory*, 2008) argues that at the time of the novel's publication, the genre of mother-daughter stories occupied a high place in literary circles; many of the novels in this category were appearing on the bestseller lists. Elliott also points to the escalating interest in stories by and about women from traditionally underrepresented groups and backgrounds. Unlike some of the feminist writers of the 1970s—Marge Piercy, Alice Walker, and Marilyn French, for example—who focused on the political underpinnings of and solutions to the cultural oppression of women, women writers of the 1980s were more interested in portraying the emotional and psychological intricacies of family relationships, particularly those between mother and daughter. These features attracted an expanding readership.

Another critic, Wendy Ho, points to the diversity of the increasing population of Chinese immigrants in the United States and speculates that among this group would be many readers experiencing the frustrations and social restrictions of "the newcomer" and "the outsider," individuals who would be drawn to stories about people facing similar dilemmas. In her book, *In Her Mother's House*, Ho cites readers' letters to Tan thanking her for writing so accurately about *their own* lives. One example is a letter from a Missouri teenager who describes her first experience of ethnic pride:

> I had never read a book like yours that I could relate to—from the dumplings that were made with the expert twist of chopsticks to the ways the "formica table was wiped down twice after dinner." . . . A few ignorant students mocking me would always cause me to wish that I had blonde hair instead of dark brown. . . . You wrote many beautiful things in your book that made me realize that I was lucky to have two cultures [,] that some traits in the Oriental culture could never be traded for an American one. (Ho 52)

Ho also cites other letters, each expressing a variation of the same message: Until I read Amy Tan I thought I was the only one who had these thoughts (about mothers and being Chinese). Drawing on her own readings and that of others (Ien Ang, 1985), Ho attributes this particular kind of popularity to what she calls the novel's "emotional verism," a representation of subjective experience, "a form of psychological reality, or an inner realism, rather than a reality based solely on an externally perceptible (social) reality" (Ho 51, 245).

Amy Tan had her own explanation for the novel's appeal:

> I think I wrote about something that hit a lot of baby boomer women whose mothers have just recently died or may die in the near future. They felt that their misunderstandings, things that had not been talked about for years, were expressed in the book. . . . [I know many mothers] who gave the book to their daughters, and daughters, who gave the book to their mothers, and marked passages of things they wanted to say. (Tan interview, *Poets and Writers* 19, no. 5: 24–32)

Tan contributed to her book's popularity by deliberately avoiding the use of "fancy five-dollar words"; this quality of accessibility combined with Ho's theory of "emotional verism" continues to draw millions of readers to Tan's first and subsequent novels.

Still, it is precisely Tan's popular success that has made her controversial in some academic circles and with some feminist critics. In her essay "Sugar Sisterhood," Sau-ling Cynthia Wong calls *The Joy Luck Club* a

> crossover hit by a female ethnic writer . . . [which] straddles the worlds of "mass" literature and "respectable" literature, stocking the shelves of airport newsstands as well as university bookstores, generating coffee table conversations as well as conference papers. (Wong, *The Ethnic Canon*, ed. Palumbo-Liu, 175)

Wong's concern about the novel is that "through acts of cultural interpreting and cultural empathy," Tan has created what Wong calls "the persistent allure of Orientalism" to persuade readers that they are "in touch" with the exotic (Wong 181). Wong warns that this element of Tan's writing may undermine the authenticity of her portrayal of Chinese Americans.

Another perspective comes from Patricia P. Chu, who writes in *Assimilating Asians* (2000) about "the utopian myth of the immigrant's Americanization" that underlies Tan's novel. Immigrants arrive believing in the promise of the United States as a land of opportunity:

> In the immigration myth, immigrants abandon an old world, which . . . has become incomplete, disordered, or intolerable, to brave the journey to America . . . [the] promised land of greater economic and social opportunity. . . . Although the immigrant may encounter substantial difficulties . . . he or she typically overcomes these difficulties by remaining true to the initial dream of American society's fairness and openness, working hard, and looking forward to the greater success and assimilation of his or her American-born children. This narrative typically emphasizes the power of the immigrant's agency . . . and denies that obstacles such as racism or economic exploitation are systemic or insurmountable. (Chu 143)

In a later essay published in *Asian North American Identities* (Ty and Goellnicht, eds., 2004), Chu worries that in Tan's novel, "Asia is portrayed as a tragic, ahistorical arena for the spectacle of female suffering, and America as the site of the Asian mothers' redemption through their own modernization and their daughters' assimilation" ("To Hide Her True Self" 63). This view suggests that some of the popularity Tan enjoys with non-Asian-American female readers is self-serving, that reading her novel provides a "feel-good" experience of American culture as superior and progressive while Asian culture is portrayed as primitive and oppressive.

In contrast, Magali Cornier Michael explicitly resists the "feel-good" explanation for the novel's popularity. In *New*

Visions of Community in Contemporary America (2006), Michael praises *The Joy Luck Club* for its emphasis on the cultural importance of interdependence and community building associated with the Asian, specifically the female Asian immigrant perspective over the "self-interested [and] market-driven notion of 'individualism'" associated with Western, particularly American, ideologies (39).

This debate about the status of Tan's novel—should it be accepted in the canon of American classics or appreciated only as a commercial popular success?—and about the irreconcilably different readings of the immigrant experience continues to attract more readers and critics and has become more spirited and complex with the publication of subsequent Tan novels.

Some information about the history behind Tan's novels will help the reader understand why her Chinese immigrant mothers and American-born offspring respond as they do to life in the United States. For nearly a century—from the middle of the 1800s to the conclusion of World War II—China, with its huge landmass and abundant resources, was coveted by several imperialist powers, including Russia, Japan, and the United States. The day-to-day social reality for most of the Chinese population during this period was consistently impacted by whatever internal hostilities, famines, migrations, revolutionary turbulence, and widespread oppression were being perpetrated by these imperialist interests.

Additionally, under the Confucian social structure, Chinese women were subject to the controlling influences of the "Three Obediences" and the "Four Virtues." Women were instructed to obey first their fathers, then their husbands, and, as widows, their eldest sons. The Virtues decreed that a woman's behavior must always be chaste, undemanding, and courteous, and her entire life was expected to be devoted to family and domestic duties (see Ho 150). During their years of childhood and young womanhood, the four mothers in the novel lived under these feudal traditions. When the determined women arrived in the United States, they brought with them the family-supporting habits and virtues of their native culture but also the painful memories of tacit suffering and oppression. After World War

II, the United States was a generally welcoming immigrant nation, but a pervasive and unresolved racism was undeniably an ongoing obstacle for many newcomers.

Discussing the novel in her book *Between Worlds: Women Writers of Chinese Ancestry* (1990), Amy Ling focuses on Tan's immigrant women, these "women warriors"—the term comes from an earlier Chinese-American novel, Maxine Hong Kingston's *The Woman Warrior* (1976). Ling discusses these women's experiences by using the term "double consciousness" created by W.E.B. Du Bois to describe the black person's experience. Du Bois said the black person was "always looking at [himself] through the eyes of others . . . [who look on] in amused contempt and pity" (*The Souls of Black Folk*, 1903, 45). Ling makes the additional point that this feeling of alienation is exacerbated for the Chinese immigrant by having two countries to call "home." She quotes from the scene in Tan's novel when Lindo Jong tells her daughter, Waverly: "When you go [back] to China . . . you don't even need to open your mouth. They already know you are an outsider. . . . They know you do not belong" (*TJLC* 253). Considered too "Chinese" in one place, too "American" in another, Ling calls this experience a "feeling of being . . . totally at home nowhere" (105). For a population, including not only Chinese immigrants and their American-born children but immigrants from anywhere, confronting such a reality, Amy Tan has made an inestimable contribution. She is among the first to bring forward so many previously muffled or silenced immigrant voices—individuals speaking powerfully and poignantly about their efforts to form new identities and communities in an alien and not always welcoming new homeland.

The Joy Luck Club is a story about stories. Storytelling has its roots in the tradition of oral narratives in ancient cultures, particularly associated with the women and children from these early societies. In the form of legends, myths, cult secrets, superstitions, and cautionary tales, oral narratives served various collective and personal needs. Telling stories about disorderly and threatening forces helped create a sense of having some control over them; sharing tribal wisdoms and warnings increased the chances for collective survival; and repeating the stories of marginalized and oppressed peoples helped to ensure an authentic recording of history.

Amy Tan knows this tradition, and, in writing *The Joy Luck Club*, she has become a major participant in the cultural changes that have elevated the value and purpose of stories and bestowed dignity and legitimacy on the storytellers. Holocaust memories, old slave stories, transformative childhood memories, individual accounts of labor movement and civil rights struggles, and the experiences of combat are newly valued as part of authentic and living history. The historian and cultural critic Hannah Arendt once wrote: "Storytelling reveals meaning without committing to the error of defining it."

Two years after *The Joy Luck Club* was published, Tan described in an essay for *Life* magazine her response to an old photograph of her mother, grandmother, aunts, and cousins:

> When I first saw this photo as a child, I thought it was exotic and remote . . . [without any] connection to my American life. Look at their bound feet! Look at that funny lady with the plucked forehead. The solemn little girl was in fact my mother. And leaning against the rock is my grandmother, Jing-mei. . . . This is also a picture of secrets and tragedies. . . . This is the picture I see when I write. These are the secrets I was supposed to keep. These are the women who never let me forget why stories need to be told. (Tan, "Lost Lives of Women: My Grandmother's Choice." *Life*, April, 1991, p. 90)

Amy Tan has introduced the reader to four compelling and memorable mother-daughter pairs whose lives cannot be fully realized without their achieving some measure of mutual understanding and reconciliation. The portrayal of the day-by-day struggles inherent to primary relationships—the false starts and misunderstandings, the exploitation of others to fulfill personal agendas, the intrusion of past events onto present lives, impulses to blame and forgive—is Tan's central subject in *The Joy Luck Club*. Her achievement as a novelist is centered in her compelling and persuasive depiction of mothers and daughters moving beyond the maddening and self-sabotaging dynamic between them to see, appreciate, and accept one another.

List of Characters

The Mothers

Suyuan Woo has died of a stroke just months before the meeting of the Joy Luck Club that begins the novel. The reader learns her story through the words of her daughter, Jing-mei Woo. The defining event in Suyuan's life was her flight from Kweilin to escape the invading Japanese army when, exhausted and overcome with fear, she could no longer carry her twin infant daughters and left them on the side of the road bundled in blankets with some valuables and their names written for identification. Once in the United States, Suyuan and her husband had another daughter, Jing-mei, but Suyuan had kept hidden from everyone the anguished memory of the other daughters and her undying hope to find them alive and reconnect with them. This hope provides both structure and continuity to the novel. Suyuan's first husband was a military officer during the Sino-Japanese War. After his death in combat, Suyuan met and married the kindly Canning Woo, who remains in the background with the other Joy Luck husbands until he accompanies his daughter on her trip to China to meet the sisters. Possibly to compensate for the lost possibilities in the twin's lives and to bring to fruition her belief that "anything was possible in America," Suyuan undertook a prolonged, ultimately unsuccessful and damaging effort to turn Jing-mei into a child prodigy. Jing-mei, also called June, remembers detecting a profound yearning in Suyuan, an underlying sense that for her mother "something was always missing."

As the name of her first story implies, of the four mothers, **An-mei Hsu** bears the most scars from her early years. The first memory she mentions is of being told her mother was a ghost. An-mei was deprived of her mother not because she died but because she was banished by her family for failing to follow the prescribed rules of behavior for widowed women. An-mei was affectionately cared for by her grandmother Popo, her mother's mother, but was relentlessly scorned by her and all her relatives for being her mother's daughter and was never allowed to express or receive the maternal affection she longed for. When An-mei was four, her mother (who was not named) appeared suddenly in the family home to take An-mei away with her; in the chaotic episode that ensued, An-mei was scarred when a pot of boiling soup accidentally fell on her. She later witnessed her mother suffering the demoralizing consequences of being trapped in the multiple wives–concubines hierarchy, part of the patriarchal power structure. In this oppressive setting, An-mei managed to develop a will to resist—she called it "[learning] how to shout"—and she brings this spirit with her to the United States and tries to instill it in her daughter, Rose. An-mei's first job in her new life is putting fortunes in cookies. This mirrors An-mei's struggle to make her own fortune anew in the new world she inhabits. Influenced by the Chinese belief in the importance of natural elements for a "balanced" personality, An-mei judges herself (and Rose) to be lacking in "wood," signifying a tendency to fall under the influence of others. At a critical moment in Rose's life, An-mei appears in one of her dreams happily planting vigorous "weeds" in the garden. Tan may be suggesting that both mother and daughter have acquired some of the missing "wood" quality.

Lindo Jong, born under the sign of the horse, is the most willful and competitive of the mothers. From her earliest years, Lindo had to rely on the powerful energy and determination associated with her birth animal to resist other people's plans for her life. Rigidly enforced cultural expectations prevented Lindo from escaping the early and cruel separation from her family and the suffocating marital union arranged for her at an early age, but she survived both by imaginatively harnessing and using the power of a wind she felt within her to keep her spirit alive and to imagine alternative outcomes. She finally finds a way to outmaneuver her in-laws and escape to a previously imagined future. In the United States, she takes a job making up other people's fortunes and meets An-mei. Lindo's fierce will plays out in her relationship with her daughter.

When Waverly shows a talent for chess, Lindo pushes her so hard to excel that she becomes, in effect, her own daughter's most wily and antagonistic rival. Waverly initially responds to this maternal coerciveness by accusing her mother of living vicariously through her daughter's tournament victories and later by losing interest in winning and choosing to end her competitive career. Although Waverly harms herself more than she damages her mother by forsaking her chess talent, she uses her competitive spirit to become a high-powered tax attorney. Lindo remains feisty to the end but gradually allows herself moments of vulnerability and, in her last story, is ready to listen to her daughter's advice. It is through Lindo's determination that the twins' letters are answered and their reunion with Jing-mei arranged, although all the Joy Luck mothers contribute to the plane fare.

Of all the mothers, **Ying-ying St. Clair** began her life in the most promising circumstances. Born under the sign of the tiger into a prosperous family, Ying-ying was a strong, playful, and adventurous child whose stable life and security are threatened by two traumatic events: a near-drowning and a shocking experience involving the Moon Lady at the Moon Festival. Ying-ying does not recover her memory of these events until much later in life when, as an adult, feeling lost and enduring episodes of anxiety, she remembers what she had wanted as a little girl: "I wanted to be found." She also remembers how she had started to become "like a small shadow" that no one could see. This shadow self subsequently accepted marriage to a rich, coarse, and philandering industrialist who told her he wanted to revive her "tiger spirit." In his company, however, her spirit only withers: " I did not lose myself all at once. I rubbed out my face over the years washing away my pain, the same way carvings on stone are worn down by water" (67). One of the harsh experiences weighing her down was the terrible choice she made to abort a child after learning about her husband's multiple acts of adultery. Later she accepted a different kind of husband, one more gentle but also bland and unseeing. He is so aloof that he is useless when Ying-ying begins her retreat into silence and mental illness. Hoping to save her daughter, Lena, from a lifeless marriage, Ying-ying summons the strength she associates with her birth sign, the tiger.

The Daughters

Jing-mei Woo speaks once in each section—twice for herself, twice for her deceased mother—and her narrative provides continuity throughout the novel. Jing-mei, also called June—the only daughter to have a Chinese and an English-language name—suffers unknowingly from her mother, Suyuan Woo's, crushing memory of having abandoned two daughters in China. Perhaps as a substitute for the missing daughters, Jing-mei's mother is intent on turning her daughter into the child prodigy she thinks is virtually guaranteed by the American Dream. While Jing-mei's antics, in service of her mother's desire, often seem humorous, for her the ordeal is destructive. Coerced into becoming "superlative," Jing-mei retaliates against her mother by choosing to become "mediocre" or, as she views it, to be nothing more than just herself, which meant to excel at nothing. This self-sabotaging choice leaves Jing-mei an undeveloped and unfulfilled adult, resigned to an unchallenging career as an advertising copywriter and feeling insecure in the presence of the other daughters, especially Waverly, who has a successful career, a child, and a new husband. Jing-mei, however, gets a chance for self-discovery when she makes the trip to China to carry out her mother's unfulfilled hope of reuniting with her lost daughters.

Rose Hsu, daughter of An-Mei and middle child in a family of nine children, lapses into a prolonged passivity after she fails to protect her little brother Bing from drowning during a family outing. Watching her mother's grief-crazed effort to recover Bing from the waves the next day and her subsequent loss of faith in a protective god, Rose develops a terror of having any kind of responsibility. Possibly as a consequence of such a potent change of personality, Rose marries a strong-willed man who initially enjoys his role as her "rescuer" and "decider" of all domestic questions. When Ted loses his professional confidence, he tires of making all the decisions and tires of Rose, whom he finds uninteresting, and he begins an affair with another woman. Rose chooses to consult a psychiatrist as her first step to take hold of her life. Whether Tan is suggesting that the new "religion" of psychiatry is ineffectual or that Rose herself is ineffectual in making use of its insights, the issues raised remain unresolved in the text. When Rose bravely confesses that she has come up with an uncharacteristic strategy for getting revenge against Ted, the psychiatrist yawns and ends the session. Rose becomes so tormented by her indecisiveness that she hides in bed for three days. During this time, she hears the equivalent of her mother's "shout." An-mei's old advice to herself to stand up and make her wishes known filters into one of Rose's dreams, manifesting as a feeling of excitement about planting in the garden. Plants signify the characteristic of "wood" thought to be missing in both mother and daughter— the quality of resolve or backbone sufficient to recognize what is desired and to move deliberately to make it happen. The mother's spirit is thus transmitted to the daughter and, as a result, Rose is able to tell Ted that she intends to reject his meager offer of ten thousand dollars and claim the house and gardens for herself.

Waverly Jong was given her first name by her mother, who wanted her to have a secure sense of place, perhaps because she herself was forcibly separated from her own family. Her name is borrowed from Waverly Place in the Chinatown section of San Francisco where the family lives, but it gives no hint about Waverly's personality. Waverly wavers about nothing; she is ambitious and goes after what she wants with steely determination. Her desire for power and superiority, combined with her inherited skills of calculation and manipulation, fit perfectly with her talent for playing chess. A fierce competitor, she quickly becomes the child prodigy Jing-mei is not: a national chess champion. Graciousness and humility are not among Waverly's strengths. After Jing-mei has performed miserably at a piano recital, Waverly tells her stricken friend: "You're not a genius like me." Waverly excels at school and becomes a tax attorney at a high-powered law office, but she is less successful in relationships. Realizing that she is locked in a chesslike battle with her own mother, Waverly chooses to give up the game. The tense competitiveness between them continues as Waverly reaches adulthood, until eventually the birth of a daughter and a genuinely loving second husband make Waverly more vulnerable and subsequently more appreciative of her mother.

Growing up with a mother suffering from anxiety and emotional strain, **Lena St. Clair** spends much of her childhood expecting the worst. Lena's family shares an apartment building with an Italian family for whom loud squabbling and melodramatic outbursts are not the sign of something sinister. Lena, hearing these noises through the wall, assumes the girl on the other side has been murdered. While Lena cowers, her neighbor scampers around having adventures. Somehow Lena grows up to become an intelligent and engaged woman who majors in Asian-American studies in college and marries an upbeat and self-motivated entrepreneur. The mutual need Lena and Ying-ying have for each other intensifies during a visit Ying-ying makes to the upscale home Lena lives in with her husband. In her mother's presence, Lena becomes aware of the loveless nature of her marriage and her husband's controlling influence.

Summary and Analysis

The Joy Luck Club is a narrative about narratives. It is, first of all, a novel shaped by Amy Tan's own story, and she begins with Jing-mei's story, which focuses mainly on her own recently deceased mother's life—a history she has heard recounted too many times to count. Jing-mei (June) shares, in her mother's words, the experience of living through the harsh years of the Sino-Japanese War (1937–1945). With her officer husband away fighting in the war, Suyuan Woo and members of other military families are hiding from the Japanese in the town of Kweilin. In the midst of the town's incongruously beautiful countryside, the grim sights and sounds of people and animals in pain are inescapable. To cope under these harrowing conditions, Suyuan Woo arranges for regular meetings during which she and three other women in similar circumstances can "feast" on whatever scraps of food are available and entertain themselves by playing rounds of mah jong. She calls this gathering the Joy Luck Club. The highpoint of the Joy Luck meetings seems to have been the storytelling that followed the feasting and game playing. Jing-mei recalls her mother's memories of

> [talking] into the night until the morning, saying stories about good times in the past and good times yet to come. Oh, what good stories! Stories spilling out all over the place! We almost laughed to death. A rooster that ran into the house screeching on top of dinner bowls, the same bowls that held him quietly in pieces the next day! And one about a girl who wrote love letters for two friends who loved the same man. And a silly foreign lady who fainted on a toilet when firecrackers went off next to her. (24).

Tan divides her novel into four sections, each section containing four stories, half told by the mothers and half by their daughters. Tan's intermingling of the stories creates an unusual narrative structure that allows the reader to watch from multiple perspectives how the emotional dynamic that binds mother and daughter plays out in day-by-day interactions and at different intervals in their lives. A brief fablelike story precedes each section to illuminate some aspect of the intractable tensions affecting each mother-daughter pair.

FEATHERS FROM A THOUSAND LI AWAY

The tale of a woman and a duck introduces the first section with themes the author amplifies throughout the novel: a desire to escape limitation, loss, disappointment, miscommunication, transference of hope from parent to offspring, and parental fear of rejection. The duck aspires to be more than a duck but its "success"—becoming a swan—exceeds expectations and cannot be sustained. At the customs checkpoint, the swan is whisked away by an official. Instead of taking the swan's disappearance as a warning about the danger of having impossible expectations for her daughter and herself, the woman resigns herself to living in a state of perpetual hope, which becomes only a life lived in perpetual frustration. Patricia P. Chu, a prominent critic of Asian-American literature, finds in this Chinese-American "ugly duckling" tale ideas relevant to many immigration narratives; these include:

> the old world as a place of limited possibility; the immigrant as the one duck who will not accept her appointed place in that society; America as the site of the immigrant's dream of transformation, the land of unbounded possibility. . . . The daughter's affinity for Coca-Cola and unfamiliarity with sorrow serve as shorthand for issues to be elaborated in the novel: the danger that the material comfort, even luxury, symbolized by the drinking of bubbly, unnourishing Coca-Cola will also lead to malnourished character development, a callousness and lack of imagination bred by the very prosperity, and shelter from suffering, that the mother has risked so much to offer. The story ends with the immigrant mother poised between hope that her daughter may still be brought to understand the world of

meaning symbolized by the swan's feather and fear that the moment for transmitting that legacy may never arise. (Chu, *Assimilating Asians*, 145)

THE JOY LUCK CLUB: JING-MEI WOO

When the novel opens, the daughters are in their thirties, the stage of life their mothers were in when they arrived in the United States to begin their arduous assimilation into American culture. The clash of cultures has created a range of conflicts; the traditional expectations of Chinese family culture, familiar and important to the mothers, had somehow to blend with the more flexible and permissive American lifestyle, familiar and important to the daughters.

The Joy Luck Club tradition has survived the crosscultural journey; Suyuan Woo reestablished the meetings with three other families living in the immigrant community in San Francisco. When Jing-mei begins to speak, she is talking to the same club members who have been meeting for thirty-eight years.

The Joy Luck Club is more than a social gathering; it "runs on" the women's vitality and self-regard and signals their hope and willingness to be self-assertive—all character traits each one possessed in some measure to make possible the major decision and task of leaving their homeland. The traits are also the same ones that must be nourished and sustained in order to survive in a new land. In Kweilin, as Jing-mei relates, her mother created the club because she needed an escape from the dread that permeated everyday life there. By playing mah jong, the women created for themselves the possibility of luck, which in turn gave rise to the opportunity for hope: "That hope was our only joy" (25). As a strategy for psychic survival, the club is an ingenious invention. Magali Cornier Michael writes about this particular purpose:

By choosing hope, the women assert themselves as active agents rather than passive victims, indicating not only that hope is necessary for survival but also that hope is a choice. (Michael, *New Visions of Community in Contemporary America* 45)

The club is also emblematic of the women's recognition that their survival depends on being part of a community, an idea culturally rooted in Chinese revolutionary politics and Chinese Confucianism in which the notion of collective well-being was considered more important than the success or happiness of a single individual.

Woo thoughtfully chose the new members of her club; all are Chinese immigrants, who have been providing each other with a sense of continuity from an earlier life and a shield against the alien ambiance of the fast-paced and materialistic life in the United States.

As the reader learns from their stories, all the women are burdened with memories of earlier events so traumatic as to be "unspeakable" even now, years later. These women still need and rely on one another, facing, as they are, the additional challenge of raising their daughters as they had imagined many years ago.

Emotional or psychic pain is a phenomenon of human life, and this culturally specific form of it is felt throughout *The Joy Luck Club*. Through Jing-mei's memory, the reader learns how her mother and her friends found relief from their suffering: They told each other funny stories. Suyuan explains why laughing at funny stories in the midst of unfathomable grief makes sense:

> It's not that we had no heart or eyes for pain. We were all afraid. We all had our miseries. But to despair was to . . . prolong what was already unbearable. How much can you wish for a favorite warm coat that hangs in a closet of a house that has burned down with your mother and father inside of it? (24)

Jing-mei begins her story seated at the "fourth corner" of the mah jong table, the seat customarily occupied by her mother; it is the seat associated with the east as the place where day begins and the East as the land China occupies. She is the first to speak, telling in effect two stories, first her mother's and then her own story about listening to her mother's story. After years of hearing the same story told with different but inconsequential conclusions, June assumed it was "like a fairly tale"; now, she relates hearing the true ending from her mother: the nightmarish retreat from the Japanese massacre of Kweilin inhabitants, pushing a borrowed wheelbarrow along the rutted road carrying her twin infant daughters and what belongings she could fit, fleeing from death to the point of exhaustion, abandoning everything but the children until she could no longer carry them, and leaving them by the roadside with a few valuables hidden in their blankets to entice the stranger who finds them to find them a new home. Tan conjures a powerful image of suffering in the tiny infants, bundled and abandoned on the road next to the cages of doomed ducklings "now quiet with thirst." Jing-mei reports the shock of hearing her mother's entire story and, worse, her cryptic conclusion: "Your father is not my first husband. You are not those babies."

At this first meeting of the Joy Luck Club without Suyuan, Jing-mei's father takes her aside to explain why his wife's death was caused by a brain aneurysm: "She had a new idea inside her head, but before it could come out of her mouth, the thought grew too big and burst" (19). It must have been a "very bad" idea, concludes her father, otherwise it would not have been so destructive. Suyuan's idea is not "bad," however; keeping a secret of this magnitude often has dangerous consequences, both mental and physical. The related observation that powerful emotions left unexpressed can create life-threatening tensions within and between people is relevant for all the Joy Luck "aunties" and all the mother-daughter pairs.

This early scene illuminates some of Jing-mei's aunts' anxieties and preoccupations. Auntie Lin's incorrect assumption that Jing-mei is still in school—she has not been for ten years—exposes the need Suyuan felt to conceal her daughter's unsettled state, a consequence of the mothers' competition among themselves to have the daughter with the most esteemed achievements. As Jing-mei corrects the misimpression, she takes some of the blame for the mistake: In the perennial arguments between them June "[always] told [her] mother what she wanted to hear" (37). The women's competitive impulses animate the weekly mah jong games, but the aim of winning the prize money has been replaced by the American preoccupation with the stock market where the risk-taking is shared: Everyone wins or loses in equal shares. The mothers' competition over the daughters' achievements, however, does not abate, and its destructive influence in the daughters' lives comes through in their stories.

Feelings of deprivation and disappointment are always present in the mothers' stories and interactions. Jing-mei speaks of this explicitly, recalling her mother's perennial dissatisfaction with friends and family members: "Something was always missing. Something always needed improving" (31). The mothers instinctively seek explanations and remedies in ancient Chinese philosophies that their Americanized daughters fail to see as anything more than interesting superstitions. These clashes of culture contribute to an impasse and a gulf that separates the generations, leaving the mothers, in particular, feeling bereft. The image of the swan feather possibly hints at what is missing. In the fable, only a single feather remains as a tangible sign of the mother's plan, so it is said to represent only the mother's "best intentions" rather than the fruition of her hopes. The feather stands for the meaning of the mother's life that she is desperate to convey to her daughter; the daughter, for her part, must, for reasons of her own, turn away and retreat.

At the end of the evening, June is given the astounding news that her mother's long and secret search for the abandoned daughters had been realized. The contact Suyuan had been seeking had finally been established, but her sudden death prevented her from following through. The mothers, who earlier in the evening had disappointed Jing-mei with their matter-of-fact way of referring to the death of their friend, now reveal not only their loyalty to her but their generosity as well with the announcement that Lindo had verified the contact with the now-adult daughters and all of the mothers had arranged to buy an airline ticket for Jing-mei to travel to Shanghai to meet them. The mothers are so thrilled by the idea of helping to fulfill their friend's dream that they have overlooked its impact on June who is left to absorb the shock on her own.

This opening story sets up the happy prospect of Jing-mei's trip and its symbolic value for her and for all the mothers and daughters. But for June, the news is still a shock. She is distressed by the older women's bewildered and indignant reaction to her confessed fear that she does not know her own mother well enough to describe her to the recovered daughters. "Imagine," say the Joy Luck mothers, "a daughter not knowing her own mother!" June thinks:

> And then it occurs to me. They are frightened. In me, they see their own daughters, just as ignorant, just as unmindful of all the truths and hopes they have brought to America. . . . They see that joy and luck do not mean the same to their daughters, that to these closed American-born minds "joy luck" is not a word, it does not exist. They see daughters who will bear grandchildren born without any connecting hope passed from generation to generation. (40–41)

June's disheartened assessment is accurate, as the reader comes to learn, and for the same reasons June has hinted at in her own accounting of mother-daughter communication—a central theme of Tan's novel: "My mother and I . . . translated each other's meanings and I seemed to hear less than what was said, while my mother heard more" (37).

Having lost one of their own, the Joy Luck mothers are reminded of their own mortality. One by one, each comes forward with a story about her life hoping before time runs out to achieve a real and lasting bond with her daughter, to overcome the sense of being strangers to one another. E.D. Huntley writes:

35

In the weeks following Suyuan's death, each woman finds the power and the voice to speak the shaping events of her life to her daughter, and to acknowledge her pain and disappointment at her lack of rapport with her daughter; and each daughter in turn manages to articulate to herself—if not to her mother—the questions with which she wrestles, the frustrations she has been unable to voice, the small epiphanies that occur to her as she begins to understand her mother. And, as each woman speaks, she . . . adds her voice to the collective narrative that drives the novel's forward motion. (Huntley, *Amy Tan, A Critical Companion* 43–44)

SCAR: AN-MEI HSU

An-mei Hsu, mother of Rose and the one who has just hosted the Joy Luck meeting where June learns about her two lost sisters, is the next to tell her story. She looks back to another generation and time, to 1923, when she was nine years old and living with Popo, her grandmother. An-mei recalls an unhappy childhood in a household dominated by female relatives who have banished her mother and filled her with cautionary tales about how a single instance of disobedience will cause her brains to pour out of her head.

An-mei's story illustrates the disturbing historical fact that women in feudal China were so indoctrinated by patriarchal influences that they did not hesitate to participate in the degrading and oppressive treatment of other women. An-mei's mother, who is called a "ghost" and a "worthless goose," but never by name, was once married to a scholarly man who died, leaving her with impossible choices. Wendy Ho writes:

The underlying reason [for ostracizing the mother] is the familial and societal perception that she has failed to remain an honorable (faithful) widow [and declined to] commit suicide, which was considered an ideal option for a woman in her predicament. (Ho 151)

Ho also points to the memory An-mei has as a little girl hiding from the watchful gaze of her father, the revered patriarchal figure whose portrait hangs prominently on the wall. Despite the loving attention An-mei receives from Popo, she has internalized her relatives' message concerning what her culture condones and condemns.

An-mei also relates her frightful experience of being burned on the neck when a pot of boiling soup spilled on her in the commotion created when her mother returned to claim her. Two years later, the scar is still there, and she describes it with an image emblematic of the suffering all the mothers silently carry:

> my scar became pale and shiny and I had no memory of my mother. That is the way it is with a wound. [It closes] in on itself, to protect what is hurting so much. And once it is closed, you no longer see what is underneath, what started the pain. (47)

An-mei's mother returned again, this time to attend her dying mother. She also succeeded in persuading An-mei to leave with her and in preventing the family from stopping them, but none of these dramatic events occurred before Popo died and not before An-mei's mother made a ritualistic gesture believed to have healing powers; she cut from her own arm a piece of flesh and added it to the soup.

THE RED CANDLE: LINDO JONG

Lindo Jong tells a story in which the power that societal expectations have over a young girl in China is felt almost like an invading force. When Lindo was two years old, the village matchmaker visited her family accompanied by the mother of the boy who was to be her future husband. Lindo remembers the penetrating eyes of the future mother-in-law peering deeply into her to eradicate any of her own ideas about her future life. Robbed first of her future, then of her family, at the age of twelve, Lindo was separated from her family when a flooding Fen River forced them to abandon their ruined fields and leave her with her future husband's family. Lindo's mother suffered as well, being expected by tradition to "swallow her own sorrow"; she had to speak to her daughter as if she were someone else's, "Biting back her tongue so she wouldn't wish for something that was no longer hers" (51). Lindo concealed her distress beneath a numb obedience to the same expectations, resolving not to bring shame on her family, but a rebellious voice survives to wonder silently "why [her] destiny had been decided, why [she] should have an unhappy life so someone else could have a happy one." This same voice grew with the strength of the horse, Lindo's birth sign, and as she was preparing for the dreaded ceremony that would forever unite her with Tyan-yu, she had an epiphany forecasting her triumph:

> I . . . looked in the mirror . . . surprised at what I saw.
> I had on a beautiful red dress, but what I saw was even
> more valuable. I was strong. I was pure. I had genuine
> thoughts inside that no one could see, that no one could
> ever take away from me. I was like the wind. . . . I made a
> promise to myself: I would always remember my parents'
> wishes, but I would never forget myself. (58)

This spirit of self-affirmation that Lindo Jong summons gets her to the United States and reorients her life toward a different and self-determined destiny. To accomplish this feat, she made a clever use of storytelling: She invented a wild tale about other people's destinies in order to escape from their control over hers. Lindo did not escape unscathed, however; she bore the harsh effects of being silent and silences when she wanted to speak of enduring the arbitrary loss of her mother. This harshness turns up years later to different effect in Lindo's fierce competitiveness with and about her daughter, Waverly.

In Ben Xu's discussion of *The Joy Luck Club*, he calls Lindo a "person of 'two faces,'" i.e., a "detached, bemused, ironic observer . . . of one's own situation." The development of this façade protects against the pain of not being in control of one's destiny and against the futility of resisting. Xu then points out that "Chinese Taoist culture helps to maintain this kind of victim mentality because it reinforces a passive if not fatalistic attitude toward life" (Xu, "Memory and the Ethnic Self," *Memory, Narrative, and Identity*, 270). This observation applies to all of Tan's immigrant women but not in the same measure. Lindo "[would] never forget herself," unlike Ying-ying who allowed herself to become "like a shadow."

THE MOON LADY: YING-YING ST. CLAIR

Unlike Lindo Jong, Ying-ying St. Claire began life in promising circumstances, with caring adults, freedom to imagine and play, and a stable, tradition-rich community. She had energy and curiosity and no fear of the risk and randomness in the life around her: "I loved the unsteady feeling of almost falling one way then another," she says of being aboard one of the festival boats (74). Yet emotional isolation and mental illness characterize her adult life, and her story begins despairingly:

> For all these years I kept my mouth closed so selfish desires would not fall out. . . . I kept my true nature hidden, running along like a small shadow so nobody could catch me. And because I moved so secretly now my daughter does not see me. . . . And I want to tell her this: We are lost, she and I, unseen and not seeing, unheard and not hearing, unknown by others. (67)

What hints are there in her story to explain this outcome? Her childhood recollections, beginning in 1918, are an unnerving mix of happily playful and unusually disturbing experiences. On the day of the anticipated Moon Festival when she was four and old enough to attend, Ying-ying awakened to a pungent burning smell, which, she was informed, was coming from a ritual incineration of the Five Evils taking place outside her bedroom window. Her amah painfully pulled her hair into an orderly appearance and dressed her in an outfit certain to feel suffocating in the day's excessive heat. She was promised a chance to ask the Moon Lady, mysterious luminary of the festival, to grant her a secret wish but not before hearing a convoluted and intentionally guilt-inducing explanation of the difference between expressing a wish (good) and a selfish desire (bad).

The festival initially proved to be full of activity, including racing around with her lively young cousins and riding on the boat; but Ying-ying got caught up in scenes of disemboweled fish, headless chickens, and wriggling shrimp chewed alive and swallowed by her father. Something also went terribly wrong: In what seems unmistakably a psychotic moment, Ying-ying poured turtle blood on herself believing that no one would notice. Even more strange is that her mother did not come to her, either to comfort or to scold. One baffling horror follows another: Ying-ying had a near-drowning experience when she fell out of a boat, and, after being rescued by fishermen, could not find anyone who wanted to claim her. With her shadow for a companion, she watched a demeaning pageant about another abandoned female, the Moon Lady. Ying-ying's story concludes when her nightmarish evening ended: Her wish—"to be found"—went unfulfilled, and the lovely apparition of the Moon Lady was exposed as a fraud. More about Ying-ying's life is told in later stories.

Each of this first set of stories told by the Joy Luck mothers derives from childhood memories, or, as in Suyuan's story related by June, from memories of a much earlier life in China. The woman with the swan who introduces this section gives voice to the hopes each has carried from the old country to the new:

In America I will have a daughter just like me. But over there nobody will say her worth is measured by the loudness of her husband's belch. Over there nobody will look down on her, because I will make her speak only perfect American English. And over there she will always be too full to swallow sorrow! (17)

THE TWENTY-SIX MALIGNANT GATES

The daughters tell the next set of stories, though the cautionary tales that preface each section also help elicit dual mother and daughter perspectives. Collectively the narratives tell of the maddening frustration that comes from living in the grip of tenaciously held maternal hopes. The Joy Luck mother, whose instinct is to protect at all cost, instructs her daughter never to stray beyond her prescribed limits, citing dangers listed in a Chinese book called *The Twenty-six Malignant Gates*. In the story, the daughter, willfully but not unreasonably from her point of view, rejects the warning, runs off with her bike, and falls. There is, the story warns, no escape from a mother's protectiveness or from her mysterious omnipotence. Critic Jane Elliott observes:

> the mysterious knowledge associated with the Chinese book trumps the daughter's supposed agency, turning even her defiance into a means of fulfilling its prophecy: whatever action the daughter takes still ends in reinforcing both the mysterious forces of Chinese causality and the infallibility of the mother. (Elliott 149)

RULES OF THE GAME: WAVERLY JONG

Waverly Jong tells the first of the daughter stories in a way that reveals the influence of her mother. Lindo Jong's conception of herself as a force like the wind has been transmitted to Waverly as a metaphor for personal power and the wily ways both women develop and assert that power. At the church Christmas party, Waverly outsmarts Santa Claus and plots how to get the best of the donated gifts for herself. After discovering she has both zeal and talent for winning chess games, Waverly manipulates her mother into allowing her to participate in competitive tournaments. Unconsciously carrying her mother's early identification with the power of the wind, Waverly imagines it is helping her win by secretly whispering suggestions into her ear as she plays. She is also coached by her mother who has moved from being disdainful of her daughter's interest to being aggressively involved.

At nine, Waverly has become a national chess champion, but despite her natural talent and devotion to practicing clever and aggressive moves, and despite her mother's sacrifice and encouragement, Waverly cannot enjoy her success precisely because it has become too entangled with her mother's aspirations, vicarious pride, and pleasure. Tan has illustrated here an important irony of the immigrant mother–American daughter relationship—namely, that although Lindo has won her mother's potent and unspoken competition for having the most successful daughter

> [she] cannot help Waverly to manipulate the system because, for Waverly, Lindo *is* the system. Waverly's story suggests that, because the mother's power is experienced by the daughter as a threatening force, the mother cannot transmit whatever power she possesses to her daughter: instead, in keeping with the zero-sum dynamic, the mother's power immediately becomes power over rather than power shared by the daughter. (Elliott 149)

THE VOICE FROM THE WALL: LENA ST. CLAIR

Lena St. Clair, daughter of Ying-ying, also begins with a childhood memory about her mother. She tells of hearing her mother's grim story about a beggar condemned to die "in the worst possible way" who returns to drag his executioner off to an even worse fate. Recalling the prolonged suffering of Ying-ying's youth makes plausible her own fascination about the "worst way to die," and Lena's early preoccupation with "unspoken terrors" seems to reflect something of her mother's early traumas and warn against a similarly unhappy fate.

Lena describes an experience from her childhood that reenacts the scenario in the cautionary tale, but in her memory, the move she makes beyond her mother's protective boundaries—going down into the forbidden basement—is suffused with terror and suggestions of a much more serious will to self-harm. She seems to have transferred her fear of violation back to her mother in remembering:

> even as a young child, I could sense the unspoken terrors that surrounded our house, the ones that chased my mother and found her. I watched, over the years, as they devoured her, piece by piece, until she disappeared and became a ghost. (103)

Lena's memories include her father's stories about her mother's arrival in the United States. Relating these stories to a young child seems a reckless act on the part of her father, because they tell of a fate that seems insurmountable and to have been determined even before her mother had a chance to begin her new life as an immigrant. At the Angel Island Immigration Center, Ying-ying was detained for nine days until a suitable name could be invented for her category of immigrant. She was released as a "Displaced Person"; in a picture taken for the occasion, Lena saw her mother dressed in an outfit that made her look as if "she [was] neither coming from nor going to someplace" (105). It is difficult to imagine how Lena will grow into a productive and satisfying adult life.

Another feature of the cautionary tale—the feeling of being trapped by an elusive maternal power—is conveyed in this exchange Lena recalls having had with her mother:

> "You must not walk in any direction but to school and back home," warned my mother when she decided I was old enough to walk by myself.
> "Why?" I asked.
> "You can't understand these things," she said.
> "Why not?"
> "Because I haven't put it in your mind yet."
> "Why not?"
> "Aii-ya! Such questions! Because it is too terrible to consider."

Lena's predilection for imagining the worst influences how she hears the tumultuous family sounds through the thin walls of their apartment house. Lena thinks the only explanation for the girl's screams is that she has been murdered by her mother; seeing her unharmed and appearing normal the next day leaves Lena at a loss. She has been given no guidance for getting beyond her culturally determined notion of domestic behavior, so she cannot understand that her neighbors are part of a world and participate in a family dynamic in which loud yelling and other dramatic outbursts are within cultural norms and not signs of something sinister.

Lena must also live with her mother's fear that their apartment is inherently dangerous, its domestic space "unbalanced," in the language of feng shui, and likely to bring personal harm. Although it is hard to imagine, Lena must absorb more pain: she must witness her mother's descent into madness, accelerated by the birth of a little brother who is deformed and quickly dies.

HALF AND HALF: ROSE HSU JORDAN

The tension animating the first part of Rose Hsu's story has its roots in American racism. Rose's mother, An-mei, is arbitrarily suspicious of Rose's boyfriend, Ted, because he is an American, and Ted's mother exposes her phony tolerance for racial minorities when she makes her condescending appeal ("Some of my best friends are black") to Rose at the family picnic. Ted's mother also shows her careless ignorance in assuming Rose is Vietnamese ("All 'Orientals' are the same").

Rose talks about her relationship with Ted with a high degree of self-knowledge: "I was victim to his hero. I was always in danger and he was always rescuing me. . . . The emotional effect of saving and being saved was addicting to both of us" (119). This insight, however, is not sufficient to make her aspire to be stronger, more autonomous, less passive, or less like a victim.

Rose's passivity, extreme enough to look pathological, contributes to the breakup of her marriage to Ted. Why she has fallen into this pattern is suggested in the story of her little brother's death. Rose gives a harrowing description of the high-spirited trip her family of nine—two parents, seven children—takes to a beach known for being a good site for ocean fishing. The family, as Rose will always remember it at this moment, is at a high point of confidence, success, and security: The United States, her family believes, is delivering its promise, and God is rewarding his faithful followers with prosperity and good luck. The accident happens quickly. Four-year-old Bing slips off a reef and disappears under the surf.

Rose had been given responsibility for her brother; but no one, not Rose, not her parents, would have been able to help once the danger beset Bing. The shock of what happened is instant and transforming. Rose thinks about the randomness and unpredictability, about the blindness of human beings, the futile gestures made to control fate. "Thinking back, . . ." she writes, "we were all blind with the newness of this experience: a Chinese family trying to act like a typical American family at the beach" (122). Rose is as affected by her guilt over this loss as she is by its effect on her stricken mother who returns the next day after all official hope of rescue has been forsaken to stand before the waves and demand, pray, bargain, and wail for her son's return. An-mei loses her religious faith; her Bible now serves only as a prop for a broken table leg, but, like all the immigrant women, she knows how to persevere and endure. Such resolve, however, is not possible for Rose, for whom the trauma has been so great she loses faith in her own competence to be able to self-direct her life, to be able—as Ted accuses her—to take the initiative or make a decision.

TWO KINDS: JING-MEI WOO

In June's story, she remembers her mother's unwavering belief in the American Dream: Anyone could do anything; everything was possible. This logic led Suyuan to believe that by simply trying, "doing your best," Jing-mei would become a child prodigy.

But, Tan writes, "[she and her mother] didn't immediately pick the right kind of prodigy" (132). After failing to become a Chinese Shirley Temple, because her hair could not be coerced into sufficient curliness, June fantasizes about other kinds of fame and other ways of being "perfect."

Tan's description of the variety of ways to become a prodigy of any sort is amusing and disturbing at once. Dazzling feats of memorization, athletic prowess, and mastering magic tricks are contemplated and discarded. June remembers, "[After] seeing my mother's disappointed face once again, something inside me began to die" (134). "Dying" for June becomes not a literal disappearance, but a determined effort not to succeed, indeed to remain "mediocre" at everything, which, in Jing-mei's mind was mistakenly equated with "being herself" but accurately calculated to disappoint her mother.

One last effort is made: Jing-mei's mother arranges for piano lessons with a hapless old instructor named Mr. Chong. Jing-mei likens her new activity to being sent to hell but quickly learns how to outsmart "Old Chong" after discovering that he is deaf. For two full hours every day, she irreverently practices while her mother, anticipating an opportunity to show off her daughter's talents to the Joy Luck mothers, signs her up to play in a community recital. Briefly (and very poignantly), June fools herself into thinking she can perform a piece from Schumann's *Scenes from Childhood* without properly practicing it but in actuality plays so many wrong notes as to make the piece unrecognizable. In the audience, frozen into embarrassment, only Mr. Chong, who cannot hear, applauds. Jing-mei remembers her mother's "stricken" face and Waverly's smug comment: "You aren't a genius like me."

Both mother and daughter retreat from this event as if all has been lost, and from each other, as well. The tension between them escalates, merges with hostility, and explodes. Jing-mei shouts at her mother, "I wish I wasn't your daughter. . . . I wish I'd never been born." Then, remembering her mother's lost twins, she chooses to utter the least compassionate and cruelest words she can volley at her mother: "I wish I were dead! Like them!"

How does Jing-mei arrive at this extremity of cruelty and self-loathing? How did her mother not notice her daughter emotionally withering before her eyes? Jing-mei was denied the maternal love that is given for "just being herself," not for some grand accomplishment. At her daughter's words, Suyuan's mind falls back to her nightmarish flight from Kweilin and seems to collapse under its emotional weight. Retreating from the room, she appears to Jing-mei "as if she were blowing away like a small brown leaf, thin, brittle, lifeless" (142). In this scene, Tan has created another disturbing spectacle in which a daughter's chances for normal happiness are undermined by a mother's excessive aspiration, while the mother, in turn, lets go of all hope.

Almost as an afterthought, Suyuan's returning the piano to Jing-mei as a gift is mentioned. Jing-mei is hesitant about receiving it, but after a time, she brings it to her apartment and slowly takes possession by caring for it and then playing it again. The gift of the piano and Jing-mei's return to playing are unmistakable signs of some kind of resolution, but what form it will take and how it will be enacted are left unsaid.

AMERICAN TRANSLATION / RICE HUSBAND: LENA ST. CLAIR

The vignette introducing the third set of stories—four more of the daughters' reflections—is a good illustration of Jing-mei's observation about mother-daughter miscommunication: mothers hear (or see) more than what is there, daughters hear (or see) less, and both see differently. The stories that follow reveal more of the mother-daughter tension and more of the emotional cost of their estranged relationships.

Lena St. Clair, writing now from the perspective of a young married woman, is still under her mother's spell, still self-conscious in her presence, still fearful of her criticisms such as those Ying-ying makes when visiting her daughter and husband at their newly renovated house. Lena, however, is less wary about her mother's quickness to notice visible minor flaws than she is of her mother's more penetrating way of seeing beneath a surface or into a future time.

Lena's portrayal of her marriage to Harold Livotny appears superficially normal except for her husband's bizarre and disturbing insistence on dividing to the penny all their expenditures, which are listed, item by item, on their refrigerator door. Harold's explanation—"As long as we keep the money thing separate, we'll always be sure of our love for each other"—is unconvincing but not completely implausible until Lena's mother also notices the inaccurate accounting for the ice cream Harold brings home every Friday night. For her own reasons (that she keeps from Harold but cannot keep from her mother) Lena does not eat ice cream but pays every week for a share of it. This tiny, singular detail, noticed and brought to light by Lena's mother, has the effect of exposing Lena to the deficiencies of her marriage. Harold has not noticed that his wife eats none of the ice cream, but, much more harmfully, he has also not noticed his wife's contribution to the marriage, her clever and helpful suggestions about his new business that aid its success. Despite these contributions, she continues to receive less of the family income for her own use than Harold does. In effect, he has not noticed—or seen—his own wife.

Earlier in the chapter Lena relates a conversation she had with her friend Rose, who is also languishing in an unsatisfying marriage. Each is searching for a remedy or an explanation and neither comes up with anything beyond anemic reasoning: that all Chinese Americans feel as they do, that an excessive amount of humility gets in the way of high expectations. Another answer may be found in Ying-ying's reply to Lena after the vase falls and breaks. In a reversal of roles, Lena foresees the bad outcome ("I knew it would break"), and Ying-ying sees a practical solution ("Then why don't you stop it?").

FOUR DIRECTIONS: WAVERLY JONG

Waverly's story, following Lena's, also deals with mothers and marriage. Waverly has arranged to take her mother to lunch at a favorite restaurant hoping to share news of her plans to marry again, but, as anticipated, the mother-daughter tensions surface instantly, and Waverly must postpone her announcement.

In the scene that follows the restaurant "disaster," Lindo makes her first visit in months to Waverly's apartment. At the restaurant she found nothing to praise and only criticism for the food, service, and accommodations. Knowing what she does about her mother's almost compulsive need to find fault, Waverly, by inviting this compulsively critical presence back to her apartment, performs an act of courage—all the more so when it becomes evident that Waverly is deliberately seeking her mother's approval of her choice of lifestyle and, especially, of her new husband. Lindo has already demonstrated her almost witchlike powers of using a few withering glances and comments to reduce an intelligent and hardworking man—Lindo's childhood sweetheart and first husband—into a lazy and stingy playboy.

Waverly is not the most easily likeable of the Joy Luck daughters—having inherited some of her mother's hard-edged and manipulative personality—but the reader follows her story sympathetically, as, with trepidation, she leads her mother through the rooms hoping she will notice and take pleasure in the signs of happy domestic chaos in the scattered toys, running shoes, and barbells and especially the mingling of her clothes and possessions with Rich's in the bedroom. But Lindo's negativity prevails: She does not notice; she cannot bring herself to acknowledge the signs of her daughter's new life and new intimacy. She does not *see* the daughter before her.

Recalling Lindo's experiences as a child, specifically her clever maneuvering to avoid having her life defined by others in order to survive as a person with will, intention, and purpose—a person, in other words, worthy of being *seen*—the reader notes how effectively she has transmitted her energy and willfulness to her professionally successful daughter. For Lindo, such a personality brought liberation; here, these same qualities bring about grave consequences for the personal life of both mother and daughter.

Lindo's show of indifference to Waverly's new life sends a shock of pain through her daughter; Waverly likens it to a jolt of electricity that sparks another memory. Like Jing-mei, who slowly lost her sense of herself after failing to become the prodigy her mother frantically tried to make her into, Waverly loses her love of chess when she unwittingly finds herself competing, as if in a chess match, with her own mother. The stakes in this psychological game are high: not trophies and not less than Waverly's sense of her own worth. She remembers feeling the terror that accompanies her recognition that "[she is] no longer a prodigy . . . she had lost [her] gift and turned into someone quite ordinary."

Among the Joy Luck mothers, Lindo's maternal power is unmatched. Tan, however, has not created a villain in this character, nor in any of the other Joy Luck mothers despite the harmful effects their manipulations and unachievable expectations have on their daughters. Tan allows them to tell their stories in such a way that readers hesitate to find fault or willingly suspend judgment.

The conclusion of Waverly's story shows everyone at their best. Becoming the mother of "perfect" Shoshana and experiencing Rich's "embarrassingly romantic" and "unconditional love" for her, Waverly has become more than a polished and ambitious professional in a tax attorney office. She has become vulnerable and acquired a capacity for self-awareness, an interest in *seeing* herself with some degree of objectivity. She marvels at her willingness to let Rich see "[her] darker side, [her] meanness . . . pettiness [and] self-loathing—all the things [she'd] kept hidden" (175).

These achievements of perspective and character, however, do not get in the way of her native talent for cleverly manipulating things to her advantage, in this case, using her mother's competitiveness and pride in cooking skills to get herself and Rich invited to dinner. Despite everything, the evening ends in another failure although this one is tinged with comic relief (partially in the form of Rich's unintended gaffes) and mainly free of Lindo's caustic disdain.

The next morning, with "enough anger to fend off a thousand flying cleavers," Waverly goes to her parent's apartment to announce that she is getting married. But not a single "flying cleaver" greets her; instead she finds her mother, vulnerable and small in her sleep, and already knowing her daughter's intentions. Unarmored by the unexpected early morning visit, Lindo even lapses into affectionate maternal language, astounding Waverly by addressing her with her childhood name, "Meimei." "Oh, her strength! her weakness!—both pulling me apart," Waverly tells herself, overcome by this display of mutual vulnerability and affection. Lindo, similarly affected, takes the moment for the long-awaited opportunity to tell her daughter a story, one about her own history, so she will know where all her "strength" and "almost all [her] good stuff" comes from.

The fragile nature of the understanding they have achieved is briefly threatened by an amusing (to the reader) confusion over the difference between "Taiwan" and "Taiyuan," but mother and daughter have arrived at a new emotional and psychic space and the awkward moment passes.

In Waverly's epiphany, she sees herself—a scared child, an impotent pawn frightened especially of her own mother—and she sees her mother, once the queen of the chessboard, no longer scary, but herself scared, diminished, and vulnerable. Gloria Shen writes about this passage:

> The sharing of cultural experience between mother and daughter through the device of storytelling transforms the naïve, self-protective daughters, who try hard to move away from, or surpass, their ethnic roots, into the mature daughters who are appreciative of their mother's Chinese ways . . . with . . . new consciousness, the mature daughter sees her mother in a new light. (*International Women's Writing* 242)

Shen quotes Waverly's words from this scene to make her point:

> in the brief instant that I had peered over the barriers I could finally see what was really there: an old woman, a wok for her armor, a knitting needle for her sword, getting a little crabby as she patiently waited for her daughter to invite her in. (*TJLC* 184)

Shen continues:

> The daughter's defiance turns out to be baseless, and the "scheming ways" of the mother who seemed relentless in her pursuit of her daughter's weakest spots prove to be unfounded. (Shen 242)

Waverly's story ends with the transformative power of her epiphany. The formerly unthinkable becomes the affectionately anticipated and wholly possible: Lindo with the newly married Rich and Waverly taking seats together on a plane to China, "moving West to reach the East."

WITHOUT WOOD: ROSE HSU JORDAN

Rose's story—begun with another account of an omnipotent mother and the daughter's acts of rebellion against her that only emerge in the safety of nighttime dreams—is about the necessity for a real rebellion she must initiate against her husband, Ted, and the demeaning image she allows him to have of her. A confession to her psychiatrist of an imagined but daringly humiliating act of retribution produces for Rose the classic and most unsatisfying dismissal: "It seems you have been experiencing some very powerful feelings. I think we should talk about them next week" (189).

Rose has divulged in her earlier story that after Ted lost his malpractice suit he announced his desire to end the marriage, but now she is dealing with his urgent request for a settlement because, as she soon learns, he has started a relationship with another woman and plans to remarry. This information is too burdensome for Rose; she cannot comprehend all the implications or decide on a course of action. She has discovered one of the unpleasant aspects of the American way of life: the tyranny of too many choices.

Rose, however, has no experience deciding for herself and the thought of doing so sends her into three days of medication-induced sleep. No hint is given about why she is suddenly able to make a brave decision, but, in a telling reversal of past patterns, Rose's mother awakens her from a nightmare, rather than causing it. Inexplicably, Rose has acquired a quantity of "wood," which Chinese folklore regards as essential for standing straight and tall and defending oneself. Ted comes to the door anticipating quick cooperation from Rose, but Rose returns the papers unsigned and announces her own intention to claim the house and remain living there.

BEST QUALITY: JING-MEI WOO

In the wrenching scene described by June in her previous story, in which she screamed at her mother about wishing to be dead, Suyuan Woo made a final effort to maintain control of herself and the family legacy before she retreated, defeated and diminished by her daughter's hurtful words. "Only two kinds of daughters," her mother had shouted, "Those who are obedient and those who follow their own mind! Only one kind of daughter can live in this house. Obedient daughter!" (142).

That scene occurred nearly three decades earlier, but its influence can still be felt in the story Jing-mei tells about the Chinese New Year dinner her mother serves in their home just two months before her sudden death. At thirty-eight, Jing-mei has not found a life or a love she can count on or even a job she can take pride in. Although she no longer lives with her parents, her workplace is only six blocks away from their apartment, and one senses how adrift she still is, unconnected to anything that matters.

During dinner, Waverly makes dismissive comments about June's hair and hairdresser, unprovoked by any words from Jing-mei. In the tense conversation that follows, about an unpaid bill for a copywriting job Waverly's firm hired Jing-mei to do, Jing-mei suddenly remembers the cruel and dismissive words Waverly said to her after her mangled performance of the Schumann piano composition: "You aren't a genius like me." The humiliation she endured from that failed long-ago effort to be a child prodigy, hidden all these years like the wound covered by scar tissue in An-mei's arm, briefly resurfaces, and when Jing-mei feels her mother joining the implied criticism, she feels herself "starting to flail, tossed without warning into deep water, drowning and desperate" (205). One has the sense that Jing-mei often finds herself in this dark and paralyzing place; she is the daughter most in need of rescue.

Again, an inadvertent remark breaks open a deadlocked relationship. Alone in the kitchen after the guests leave, Jing-mei and her mother get into a discussion about the crabs served for dinner. Jing-mei wonders what would have happened if one of the guests had eaten the crab her mother decided later to discard as inedible. But applying her unique insight, Suyuan knows that only Jing-mei would have chosen that crab and somehow Jing-mei knows her mother has complimented her. In the tiny flow of affection that follows, Suyuan takes off the gold necklace with the jade stone she is wearing and gives it to Jing-mei: "When you put [this] on your skin . . . you know my meaning. This is your life's importance."

About this scene, Wendy Ho writes:

The jade pendant is an emblem of the experiences and stories of Chinese American mothers and daughters that have often been erased, distorted, or devalued in society. This pendant, in the final story of the book, speaks also to the value of reclaiming a living covenant between a deceased mother and an adult daughter. June [Jing-mei] begins the difficult process of coming to know a woman and a legacy she has long neglected and misunderstood. (Ho 233)

QUEEN MOTHER OF THE WESTERN SKIES / MAGPIES: AN-MEI HSU

To experience the purpose and impact of Tan's novel it is essential to read each story in the context of all the others, keeping in mind not only how the daughters must confront and overcome the burdens—inherited and inflicted—that come from having been born to these particular mothers but also how they carry forward the unresolved questions their mothers have suffered with—in some cases triumphantly, in others, disastrously.

For example, in An-mei's story that begins the final set of mother stories, the bond of pain that unites An-mei with both her mother and her daughter, Rose, is reinvoked. Jane Elliot refers to this bond as a kind of mother-daughter "fusion" and observes that, as indicated by An-mei's story about living first without and then with her ostracized mother, "pain is the defining element in their relationship"(147). An-mei recalls that after her mother tells her about the turtle in the pond's warning against crying, because "tears do not wash away your sorrows. . . . They feed someone else's joy" (217), she looks up to see her mother is crying and thinks, almost defeated, "that this was our fate, to live like two turtles seeing the watery world together from the bottom of the little pond" (217). Elliott writes:

> the tears of one merely prompt the tears of the other, locking them in an endless cycle of mutually consuming grief that threatens to drown them both. If daughters represent the abstract future and mothers the painful and particular past, mother/daughter fusion in suffering figures an overload of past pain such that the abstract, painless future is eradicated entirely. To put it another way, mother/daughter fusion works so well that the daughter's identification with the mother's pain eradicates her own access to futurity. (Elliott 147)

Returning to An-mei's final story, the reader learns how, as a child, she witnessed the struggle for power and favor among Wu Tsing's various wives. Without fully understanding the horror of what she was witnessing, she saw her mother being tricked by the infertile Second Wife into becoming one of Wu Tsing's concubines and bearing, against her will, a son for the Second Wife to present to Wu Tsing as her own. An-mei is pained watching her mother suffer in this new situation. She says, "I wanted my mother to shout at Wu Tsing, to shout at

Second Wife. . . . But my mother didn't even have the right to do this. She had no choice"(238). Later, after witnessing her mother's prolonged suicide, An-mei chose to make a small gesture of rebellion. She displayed the fake pearl necklace Second Wife had given her as a sign of her phony affection and crushed it under her feet: "And on that day, Second Wife's hair began to turn white. And on that day, I learned to shout" (240).

This memory surfaces in An-mei's current story because she is concerned about her daughter's marriage and the painful divorce she is going through. An-mei remembers how she was raised according to Chinese custom—"I was taught to desire nothing, to swallow other people's misery, to eat my own bitterness"—and broods over her own daughter's passive response to her marital unhappiness. "No choice! No choice!" her daughter insists. An-mei wants to break with the past; she wants Rose to choose a different solution, a self-motivated path away from suffering. She thinks, "[Rose] doesn't know. If she doesn't speak, she is making a choice. If she doesn't try, she can lose her chance forever" (215).

Rose has already related this part of her story. In an earlier telling, she had been trying to find the right response to the anticipated loss of her comfortable life with Ted, but such grim prospects send her to bed for three days of escape via medication-induced sleep. Concerned, An-mei wakes her with a phone call and a new piece of advice: "I am not telling you to save your marriage, I only say you should speak up" (193). When Ted calls with his ultimatum, Rose has an epiphany and experiences a rush of wild laughter brought on by a long-awaited liberation and release. In her hard-won moment of clarity, she decides not to automatically succumb to Ted's wishes to slowly and, for him, conveniently disappear from his life. She will not be content with the check for ten thousand dollars and his banal best wishes. Instead, deciding to speak up ("I learned to shout"), she announces her intention to stay in the house and to take possession of the gardens for which she has acquired a special appreciation. Ted sputters a response which Rose, using the same Chinese word her mother used for describing the spurious effect of "a psyche-atricks," calls *hulihudu* ("confused"). That night, she has a dream in which her mother and a formerly scary man, Mr. Chou, are planting weeds in some window boxes. It is a good omen.

WAITING BETWEEN THE TREES: YING-YING ST. CLAIR

Ying-ying's desolate ruminations take place in the guest room of her daughter Lena's house. Compared to the sprightly and adventurous little girl she was before her demoralizing encounter with the Moon Lady at the festival, Ying-ying is a diminished, almost ghostlike woman. In her initial thoughts, she expresses the disappointment all the Joy Luck mothers feel in regard to their daughters. She thinks:

> I love my daughter. She and I have shared the same body. There is a part of her mind that is part of mine. But when she was born, she sprang from me like a slippery fish, and has been swimming away ever since. All her life, I have watched her as though from another shore. (242)

Only the most fragile of emotional bonds unite this mother and daughter pair. Her mispronunciation of Social Security as "so-so security" is amusing, but the innuendo of inadequacy is poignant and may explain the extra money she receives from her daughter and son-in-law. Taking this monthly supplement gets in the way of her desire to speak truthfully to them and also serves to remind the reader of the disadvantage immigrants have trying to master the language.

Ying-ying was born into the most privileged family situation possible for Chinese women at that time, and for a while she enjoys feeling free to make some decisions for herself. It is discouraging, then, to hear her recall her life after childhood as mainly bleak and devoid of the satisfactions of love and motherhood. Her first husband was arrogant and coarse, displaying his sexual intentions to her by savagely splitting open a ripe watermelon. After she learned of his many infidelities, she arranged to abort the son she was carrying and have the body thrown into a lake.

Ying-ying yearns to share the burden of this memory with Lena because doing so would give her the sense of being visible, of having validity as a person, but so far she has not been able to bring herself to this level of confidence. This acknowledgement of weakness reminds Ying-ying that she was born in the year of the tiger and is supposed to have—and once did have—the tiger's fighting spirit.

Ten impoverished years passed before Ying-ying felt ready to reclaim enough of her spirit to begin a new life. She moved to Shanghai, adopted a fashionable appearance, and worked as a saleslady in a clothing shop. She was courted by a bland American man, Clifford St. Clair, who worked as an exporter of Chinese clothes. After learning that her husband has been murdered by one of his jealous paramours and after vacillating about St. Clair for four years, Ying-ying finally succumbs to his moderate charms and decides to marry him and live in the United States. As she sits in the tiny guest room, overhearing Lena and Harold's conversation downstairs, using "words that mean nothing," Ying-ying decides to cease being a "ghost" of herself by reclaiming her tiger's spirit and telling her real story to her daughter. In this pivotal moment, Ying-ying is drawing on the tradition of the talk story, an oral tradition summoned to transmit family and community wisdom between generations, ensure the survival of family histories, and, specifically, to provide a succinct way for a parent to pass down warnings, insights, secrets, and confessions to his or her offspring with the hope of giving strength to descendents. Talk stories are made up of "words that mean something." Making this gesture, Ying-ying thinks, will restore her own *chi*, her spirit, and bestow on Lena the same tiger spirit that is rightfully hers.

Ying-ying, briefly a free spirit in her youth but mainly silenced by circumstances thereafter, is poised to speak for herself for the first time in many years, and Lena, with her mother's encouragement, has just spoken up for herself, too, although it appears as only about a trivial matter: Harold's ice cream she is expected to pay for in their strange family accounting system. There is certainly the promise that both mother and daughter are on the verge of taking responsibility for their own voices, ready to claim their lives for themselves.

For some readers and critics, this apparent resolution has become controversial and an example of some of the problems with Amy Tan's writing in general. Those of this opinion question the credibility of some of the author's observations. One version of this challenge is expressed in a passage by critic Patricia P. Chu:

> Tan's work at times celebrates the tragic beauty of maternal or filial sacrifice and at other times asks us to believe that mothers who have been portrayed as destroyed by oppression, as having lost their selves, may yet bequeath to their daughters a useful legacy of strength and wisdom. For instance, the character of Ying-ying St. Clair is portrayed as a ghost of her spirited girlhood self, having survived an abusive marriage, war, and abortion in China, followed by marriage to an uncomprehending Westerner, emigration, a miscarriage, and a nervous breakdown in the U. S. Yet the novel asks us to imagine Ying-ying transmitting her ineffable "tiger spirit" and teaching assertiveness to her unhappily married daughter, merely by telling her about her own lifetime of fairly passive suffering. . . . Not only is this psychologically implausible, but it offers a simplistic panacea—internalizing maternal support and female pride—for problems that need to be addressed interpersonally and structurally. (Chu, *Asian North American Identities*, Ty and Goellnicht, eds., 63)

DOUBLE FACE: LINDO JONG

In the brief reverie that precedes her last story, Lindo Jong comments on an unexpected development in Waverly's self-image, her recently stated preference for appearing "Chinese" now that the look has become fashionable, a somewhat exasperating development after all the years Lindo tried to instill "the Chinese way" in her reluctant, increasingly Americanized daughter. It is an irony apparently missed by Waverly but not by Lindo, who goes on to confess to herself:

> It's my fault she is this way. I wanted my children to have the best combination: American circumstances and Chinese character. How could I know these two things do not mix? (254)

In this poignant lament, Lindo is speaking for all the Joy Luck mothers. They, too, would have had the same response to their daughters as Lindo does to Waverly when she dismisses one of her mother's suggestions: "Don't be so old-fashioned, Ma; I'm my own person." Lindo thinks: "How can she be her own person? When did I give her up?"

Lindo's last story begins during a visit with her daughter to an elegant beauty salon—the proper setting for a literal examination of faces, appearance, and the overriding theme of the novel, the formation and understanding of one's identity. Despite their recently increasing mutual understanding, mother and daughter exhibit here more of the tension that perennially flares between them. Lindo thinks her hairdo is adequate for Waverly and Rich's upcoming wedding, but Waverly wants something different for her mother, something fashionable, not too "kinky or weird." Mainly, as Lindo knows, her daughter is worried that all Rich's "important lawyer friends" will see the mother of the bride as a "backward old Chinese woman."

Another irony, not noted by either mother or daughter, is the way Waverly feels the need to speak for her mother "as if," Lindo thinks to herself, "I had lost my hearing"; "before I can even speak," "as if I cannot understand English," and "as if I were not there," Lindo observes. This is the same Lindo who came to the United States with many painful memories of hearing others speak for her, other voices deciding which household she would grow up in and which man she would marry.

Irony begets more irony. These observations make the issues of identity and communication acutely personal and painful for Lindo. Sitting in the salon with Waverly, who is speaking for her, and Mr. Rory, the hairdresser, who is about to change the way she looks, brings up feelings of shame. Lindo responds with her "American face ... the face Americans think is Chinese, the one they cannot understand" (255). The feelings she is hiding behind the "American face" are, paradoxically, less accessible to her than those she was taught to "swallow" back in China. Not much has changed. Critic Ben Xu writes about this passage:

> The wearing of a mask is to Lindo Jong an heroic act—an act necessary for the survival of poor immigrants like herself, who feels 'it's hard to keep your Chinese face in America.' Wearing a mask means the ability to suppress one's true feelings and emotions—even to deceive—in order to be allowed to live. ... With many Chinese-Americans like Lindo Jong, survivalism has led to a cynical devaluation of heroism and to a resignation that is tinged with a bitter sense of humor. (Xu 269)

The transition to the story of her first experiences as an immigrant in the United States makes sense in this context. From the beginning she must pretend to be somebody she is not—a student of theology—and state a purpose she does not actually have—preparing to take what she learns in the United States back with her to China. She has to pay a Chinese girl raised in the United States for advice on finding affordable shelter and tricking the immigration authorities into admitting her. The girl's last instruction is to get a Chinese husband who is an American citizen.

Lindo's story of meeting An-mei at the fortune cookie factory where they both work is amusing and endearing, especially when Lindo and An-mei read the fortunes aloud with amused disbelief at their infamously comical mistranslations:

> English: "Do not fight and air your dirty laundry in public; to the victor go the soils."
> Chinese: "You shouldn't fight and do your laundry at the same time. If you win, your clothes will get dirty."

In general, the novel documents the life-disfiguring pain caused by mistranslation and miscommunication between people, but in this brief reverie, all the mistakes and awkward moments actually relieve pain by bringing people closer and making them laugh together. The sight of Lindo and the man she will eventually marry attempting to communicate in a Chinese dialect class that reduces them to telling each other, "I see cat," "I see rat," and "I see hat" is another noteworthy example. When Tin Jong, Lindo's new friend, finally proposes to her, he does so with the help of a fortune cookie that persuades him to ask: "Lindo, will you spouse me?"

Tan makes no explicit statement about the effect on Waverly of her mother's talk story, but back in the salon there is another small episode of mother-daughter reconciliation, perhaps brought on by Lindo's explaining to Waverly the origins of her name:

> Waverly . . . was the name of the street we lived on. And I wanted you to think, This is where I belong. But I also knew if I named you after this street soon you would grow up, leave this place, and take a piece of me with you. (265)

In the last scene of Lindo's story, Waverly "puts her smiling face next to [Lindo's] worried one," an impulsive gesture intended to reassure her mother that the identical shape of their noses is good because it conveys a shared trait of knowing how to appear able to get what you want—an instance of American circumstance and Chinese "trickery" working together.

A PAIR OF TICKETS: JING-MEI WOO

"In America I will have a daughter just like me," says the woman with the swan at the beginning of the novel. Throughout the narratives that follow, many references are made to the intense maternal wish of the immigrant women to replicate themselves in their daughters. They want to forge from a combination of "American circumstance and Chinese character" a redemption of their own damaged and limited lives by enabling their daughters to live undamaged and unlimited lives.

Emotional identification of this intensity is often conveyed through the imagery of blood and bones, as in "It's in the blood" and "I feel it in my bones." It is through these images that Jing-mei expresses the exhilaration of making her mother's journey for her: "my blood [rushes] through a new course" and "my bones [ache] with a familiar old pain" (267).

In all her years growing up, Jing-mei resisted the words of her mother: "Once you are born Chinese, you cannot help but feel and think Chinese. Someday you will see. It is in your blood, waiting to be let go" (267). This assertion, namely, that identity is entirely a matter of genetics, is the focus of an ongoing controversy about identity formation and about how "identity" is presented in literature and popular culture. Several critics, already cited here, are among those debating this topic. Their work is cited in the acknowledgments at the end of this volume.

Another scene from the past is introduced: Jing-mei and her father in the train traveling through China. Both father and daughter have tears in their eyes watching a

> sectioned field of yellow, green, and brown, a narrow canal flanking the tracks, low rising hills, and three people in blue jackets riding an ox-driven cart on this early October morning. (268)

This scene powerfully evokes all nostalgic homecomings; it is specific to these characters yet relevant to all.

The imagined reunion seems to occur and stand outside time; in Jing-mei's mind, her sisters have been living as eternal images, not subject to aging or even of being rescued. This trick of time and the human mind is one of many marvels Tan includes in her closing chapter. Before the actual reunion, however, there are other imagined ones: some with the twins advanced to the age of six; some in which the twins know about Suyuan's death; some in which they do not. In all of these scenarios, Jing-mei experiences herself as different identities: the daughter of the dead mother who has other daughters for whom she is alive; the daughter who had the mother her sisters only dreamed of having; the daughter with the name that means "pure essence of younger sister"; the daughter who is both oldest in one family and youngest in another; and always as the daughter who suddenly knows her familiar mother in an entirely unfamiliar way. Everything Jing-mei has understood about herself has been, in effect, tossed into the air and waiting for the right moment and place to land in a new configuration of herself.

All these changes are taking place in the imagination; when Jing-mei actually arrives in Guangzhou, the process continues as she sees herself physically among the Chinese people on the streets and groups of non-Chinese tourists: Her face shares some of the features with the Chinese natives; her height is more like that of the tourists; she knows there is a difference between Mandarin and Cantonese but can speak neither competently; her birth country has safety rules for workers, but in this Chinese city construction workers labor without work hats. There are also the shocks: What is a Hyatt Regency doing in downtown Shanghai? How did China get so "Americanized"? What does this hybridization mean?

These moments are an indirect gift from her mother—and they are lifesaving. In a way Suyuan could not otherwise have arranged, they provide Jing-mei with the possibility for self-discovery that she has missed out on. Of the four daughters, Jing-mei is the only one with both a Chinese name and an American name—Jing-mei and June. She has been both a divided and an undefined self. In the section "Best Quality," she came to an important insight: "I realized I was no better than who I was. I was a copywriter. . . . I was good at what I did, succeeding at something small. . . . I felt . . . as if I had been running to escape someone chasing me, only to look behind and discover no one was there" (207). This insight prepares her for the trip to China by making her vulnerable to even greater insights when she gets there. It is not clear how these insights will change Jing-mei's life, but it does not impact the power or effect of a novel that has shown the process of getting to the place of insight and change, particularly the process that mothers and daughters must follow. Jing-mei's and Suyuan's stories fittingly begin and conclude the novel. Jing-mei's story spans the lifetime of one of the mothers, ending with the fulfillment of that life. The fulfillment of Suyuan's life is not only enacted by her daughter, but it coincides with and makes possible the transformation of her daughter's. "The mothers do not wish to be forgotten," writes Wendy Ho (156). Jing-mei's trip ensures that her mother's life will be remembered and her own life will be worthy of remembering. Tan has shown how storytelling—about secrets kept and finally shared—can be a powerful means of attaining this growth and insight.

BEN XU ON THE SYMBOLISM
OF THE MAH JONG GAME

[T]he Joy Luck Club itself, with a magnificent mah jong table at its center, is an expression and embodiment of that survival mentality and its strategies of psychic defense. Suyuan Woo, mother of the book's first narrator, started the first Joy Luck Club in wartime Kweilin as a refugee running away from the triumphantly advancing Japanese troops. In times of trouble, everyday life became an exercise in survival, both physical and mental. If "hero" means someone who takes decisive action during a time of crisis, then for Suyuan Woo, whose life was in crisis, survival itself became a decisive action—a heroic action, albeit a pathetic and disenchanted one. In order to hang on to living, the club members in Kweilin tried to "feast," to "celebrate [their] good fortune, and play with seriousness and think of nothing else but adding to [their] happiness through winning" (11). As Suyuan herself explains: "It's not that we had no heart or eyes for pain. We were all afraid. We all had our miseries. But to despair was to wish back for something already lost. Or to prolong what was already unbearable" (11–12).

Suyuan starts the second Joy Luck Club in San Francisco in 1949. This time she is a refugee fleeing from the triumphant Communists in China. This second club is both a memory of the first club and a renewed means of survival. For those new club members newly immigrated to America, "who had unspeakable tragedies they had left behind in China and hopes they couldn't begin to express in their fragile English," the happy moments of playing mah jong are the only time they can "hope to be lucky"—"That hope was our only joy" (6, 12).

If the mah jong club reflects and is part of the Club Aunties' survival endeavor, it is not just a common sense survival that describes the difficulty of making ends meet or alludes to the fear of poverty. It expresses the perception that they are all survivors in the sense that they have lived through dark times and have emerged in the new world. It indicates the urgency to hold one's life together in the face of mounting pressures, which are seen in the dire light reflected from their memories of specific events that once victimized them in earlier times. Understanding is made necessary when one encounters the unfamiliar, the unknown, the uncanny. The process of understanding ordinarily begins with the displacement of the thing unknown toward something that is known, apprehended, and familiar. The process of understanding thus begins with an experiential shift. The domain of the unknown is shifted, by renewing the old strategy of survival, toward a domain or field presumably already mastered. All the stories included in the first section of the book are about mother-narrators's experiences of victimization. These old memories help shift the narrators, especially in an unfamiliar environment, to a growing belief that people are all victimized, in one way or another, by events beyond their control. . . .

Not only does Suyuan's early experience of extreme situations result in a defensive contraction of self, but also it transforms her relationship with her daughter into one of survival: a fear that she will lose her connection with her daughter, and that her experiences, thoughts, beliefs, and desires will have no future successors. The daughter may look like the mother, or even identify with her; and yet, the two are still worlds apart from each other. . . .

Memory is not just a narrative, even though it does have to take a narrative form; it is more importantly an experiential relation between the past and the present, projecting a future as well. It is the difference of experiential networks between Suyuan Woo and her daughter that accounts for the daughter's resistance to the mother's nagging about hard work and persistence, as well as for her confusion about the mother's constant sense of crisis.

Hard work and persistence are with the mother—and most "diligent" Chinese immigrants—less self-sufficient virtues than means and conditions of survival. These qualities are desirable to her just because she learnt from her previous experiences that they are attributes of a "winner" in life, and she is going to treat them only as such. It is only on the usefulness of these qualities that she will base her self-approval for exercising them. Even though she knows pretty well that her daughter will never get a Ph.D., she keeps telling her friends and neighbors that Jing-mei Woo is working on it. This is less a lie or wishful thinking than an expression of her survival instinct: what the mother seeks from her friends and neighbors is not the kind of approval that applauds her daughter's personal qualities, but the conviction for herself that her daughter possesses the attributes of a survivor. It is too easy to advance diligence, frugality, or whatever as Chinese ethnic qualities. What is wrong in such a view is an essentialist interpretation of these qualities as *inherent* "Chinese" attributes, and a blindness to their special relations with a particular kind of ethnic memory.

The disposition for many first generation Chinese immigrants in America to see life as a constant test of survival, to the extent that it almost becomes ethnic symbolism, is a complex mentality. It is deeply rooted in China's past of hardship and numerous famines and wars. The word in Chinese that denotes "making a living in the world" is *qiusheng*—seeking survival, or *mousheng*—managing survival. The Chinese classics are full of wisdom on how to survive, whether it be Taoist escapism, Confucian doctrine of the mean, or Legalist political trickery. The lack of religion and of a systematic belief in an after-life in Chinese culture indicates the preoccupation with the urgency of surviving in the present world. The simultaneous contempt for business (and "the rich") and love of money (in the form of thriftiness) support the view of money not as a measure of success but as a means of survival.

However, survival mentality in China has never become a symbol of nationality and ethnicity. It is part of the living conditions which have remained intact with little change throughout centuries; but it has never been mobilized and turned into what Werner Sollors, in his *The Invention of Ethnicity*, calls "kinship symbolism." Only when a Chinese person is uprooted from his or her own culture and transplanted into an alien one does he or she become aware of the fluidity, proteanness, and insecurity of his or her self. It is not until then that he or she feels the need to define himself or herself by a reference group, or even deliberately manages a certain image or presentation of self using the symbolism of survival. . . . The newly acquired ethnic awareness of being Chinese in America and the sense of urgency about the individual's and the group's preservation and survival register the waning of the old sense of a durable public world, reassuring in its definiteness, continuity, and long-tested survival strategies.

Once the imagery of confinement, insecurity, alienation, and extreme situations takes hold of the imagination of an ethnic group, the temptation to extend this imagery to lesser forms of stress and hardship and to reinterpret every kind of adversity or difference in the light of survival proves almost irresistible. Things as trifling as the Chinese way of playing mah jong, which, according to the mothers in *The Joy Luck Club*, is different from and far superior to the Jewish mah jong, is jealously guarded as a matter of immense significance. The excessive concern with being "genuinely Chinese" announces the abandonment of efforts to adapt to a mixed and heterogeneous society in favor of mere ethnic survival.

Even at the mah jong table people have to face the agony of how to survive. "We used to play mah jong," explains Auntie An-mei to Jing-mei, "winner take all. But the same people were always winning, the same people always losing." This is what life has always been: there has to be someone who is a loser and a victim. But the San Francisco Joy Luck Club Aunties reformulate their mah jong game so that it becomes, symbolically at least, a game with no losers: "We got smart. Now we can all win and lose equally. We can have stock market luck. And we can play mah jong for fun, just for a few dollars, winner take all. Losers take home leftovers!" (18).

The change in the mah jong game may appear insignificant. But it reflects the Club Aunties' view of the loser as a victim who fails to survive, and their belief that one should make every effort to defend oneself against the bruising experience of being a loser, even at a mah jong table. Such a view can alter the way competition and rivalry are experienced. Competition, whether it be in a chess game, in a piano performance, or for a

69

college degree, now centers not so much on the desire to excel as on the struggle to avoid a crushing defeat. A willingness to risk everything in the pursuit of victory gives way to a cautious hoarding of the reserves necessary to sustain life over the long haul. For Lindo Jong, her daughter's chess championship is not just proof of her talent. It is more essentially her attribute of being "lucky" and being a winner. Worldly success has always carried with it a certain poignancy, an awareness that "you can't take it with you"; but among the Chinese, glory is more fleeting than ever, and those who win a game worry incessantly about losing it.

GLORIA SHEN ON AMY TAN'S ATYPICAL NARRATIVE STRUCTURE

In *The Joy Luck Club*, important themes are repeated in the stories like musical leitmotifs and presented from slightly different angles in order to give the reader a continuous sense of life as well as a full understanding of the significance of each event. The unique structure of *The Joy Luck Club* allows the unconnected fragments of life, revealed from different but somewhat overlapping perspectives by all the "reliable" narrators, to unfold into a meaningful, continuous whole so that the persistent tensions and powerful bonds between mother and daughter, between generations, may be illuminated through a montage effect on the reader. . . .

The dissolution of unity in the traditional novel, best manifested in the "fragmentation" of the work, serves to highlight different themes that evolve around the mother–daughter relationship. . . .

Tan's storytelling technique reveals the complexity of the dark, invisible mind of cultural consciousness and subconsciousness best portrayed by the stories within stories. In *The Joy Luck Club*, Tan moves with swiftness and ease from one story to another, from one symbol or image to another. In a sense, *The Joy Luck Club* can be properly called a collection of intricate and haunting memories couched in carefully wrought stories. Tan has purposely externalized the eight characters' mental world by allowing each of them to tell her own story in a deceptively simple manner, thus allowing the reader to plunge into the mind of the characters. The motives, desires, pains, pleasures, and concerns of the characters are thereby effectively dramatized. This particular writing strategy allows Tan to transcend the conventional novelistic dichotomy of preferred "showing" and undesirable "telling." The stories thus tell us a great deal about individual characters, their reaction to each other, and their activities together. Because the stories are all told in the mothers' and the daughters' own voices, we are spared the pressing question with which the reader of a conventional novel is constantly bombarded: Am I dealing with a "reliable" or "unreliable" narrator? While immersed in particular and individual perspectives, the reader of *The Joy Luck Club* also confronts the more general and lasting concerns of many generations. Unlike Maxine Hong Kingston's *The Woman Warrior*, which relates the life experience of one woman and concentrates on one single family, the stories in *The Joy Luck Club*, with its characters and circumstances skilfully interwoven, presents a continuous whole more meaningful than the sum of its parts.

In *The Joy Luck Club*, Tan probes the problematic mother–daughter relationship in sixteen separate stories spanning two generations of eight women. Though the eight characters are divided into four families, the book itself is concerned more with an unmistakable bifurcation along generational lines: mothers, whose stories all took place in China, and daughters, whose stories deal with their lives in America. Though the mothers all have different names and individual stories, they seem interchangeable in that they all have similar personalities—strong, determined, and endowed with mysterious power—and that they all show similar concerns about their daughters' welfare. As a result, the mothers are possessively trying to hold onto their daughters, and the daughters are battling to get away from their mothers. The four mothers and four daughters are different, but their differences remain insignificant as the action of the novel is focused on the persistent tensions and powerful bonds between them.

Tan's characters are seen in both detail and outline. The first-person testimonies allow the reader to examine each of the characters closely and to develop a sense of empathy with each of them; but, at the same time, the testimonies reveal a pattern, particularly in the way the mothers and daughters relate to one another. The purpose of this treatment is obvious: to portray the mother and daughter relationship as both typical and universal.

In Tan's novel, The Joy Luck Club is a bridge uniting both space and time. The Joy Luck Club connects the sixteen intricately interlocking stories and helps to reveal and explain the infinite range and complexity of mother–daughter relationships. Within the narrative, it joins two continents and unites the experiences of the mothers and the daughters. The American daughters are alien to Chinese culture as much as they are to their mother's uncanny, Chinese ways of thinking. To the daughters, cultural and ethnic identity is possible only when they can fully identify themselves with their mothers through their maturation into womanhood. The sharing of cultural experiences between mothers and daughters through the device of storytelling transforms structurally isolated monologues into meaningful dialogues between mother and mother, daughter and daughter, and, more important, mother and daughter and coalesces the sixteen monologues into a coherent whole. While the mother and daughter relationships are unique in the ethnic context of Tan's novel, they also have a universal aspect. Indeed, all women share this experience, regardless of time and space. An-mei Hsu is puzzled by both the specific and universal qualities of the mother–daughter relationship. Raised traditionally, she was taught to swallow her desires, her bitterness, and the misery of others. Rejecting her upbringing, she tries to instill in her daughter a strong sense of self. Unfortunately, her daughter is a passive individual. An-mei Hsu is thus convinced that regardless of their respective upbringing, mothers and daughters are somehow condemned to being similar: "And even though I taught my daughter the opposite, still she came out the same way! Maybe it is because she was born to me and she was born a girl. And I was born to my mother and I was born a girl. All of us are like stairs, one step after another, going up and down, but all going the same way" (215).

Through her structural experiments with the elements of fiction and her storytelling device, and with the testimonial mode of characterization, Tan has pushed her novel beyond the merely conventional practice of the novel (to mimic the convention of the appearance of life, as done by many traditional novelists). Instead, she tries to do away with "his story" and present "her life" from the perspectives of the individual women characters in the form of loosely connected monologues. These monologues serve to translate as faithfully as possible the intricate relationship that can exist between a mother and her daughter.

Tan's extensive use of symbols and images creates a mood of expression that reveals and explains the infinite range and complexity of these mother–daughter relationships. Each of the four sections of *The Joy Luck Club* begins with a prologue, defining the theme of that section while disclosing certain aspects of the problem in the mother–daughter relationship. The first prologue contains a cluster of images that highlight the nature of this relationship in the book and summarize the whole novel. This prologue centers around an old woman who remembers that, while still in Shanghai, she bought a swan for a small sum. The swan, according to the vendor, was once a duck who had managed to stretch his neck in the hope of becoming a goose. On the boat sailing to America, the old woman swore to the swan that she would one day have a daughter whom no one would look down upon, for she would speak only perfect English. In order for this daughter to know her mother's meaning, she would give her the swan (17).

However, upon arriving in America, the swan is confiscated, and the old woman is left with only one of the swan's feathers. This feather is far too insignificant for her to convince anyone, least of all her daughter, how beautiful the swan was. Furthermore, the daughter she had hoped for has become an unsympathetic "stranger" who does not even speak her language. The prologue thus ends on a poignant note. Indeed, year after year, the mother waits for the moment when she would be able to tell her daughter in perfect American English that the feather is far from worthless, for it symbolizes all of her "good intentions" (17).

The prologue sets the tone and the reasons for the tensions and conflicts in the mother–daughter relationship. The "swan" and the "old woman" who sailed across the ocean together, "stretching their necks toward America" (17), are an emblem of the four mothers who came to the United States, hoping to give their daughters a better life than the one they had in China. The "good intentions" are clearly stated. But the mother, left with an almost worthless feather, is condemned to wait patiently many years until the daughter is finally mature enough to come back to her, to appreciate her, and to reconstruct the beautiful swan from the feather. The swan is therefore emblematic of both the mother's new life in America and, more important, her past one in China, an experience the mother wants to communicate to her daughter. However, only a mature daughter, who has overcome the psychological and cultural gap separating her from her mother is capable of coming to terms with this experience. . . .

The device of storytelling by women to women is employed extensively throughout the novel as a means to achieve various ends. . . .

Through the sharing of personal experiences, a reconciliation between mothers and daughters is reached. The daughters realize that their mothers have always had their best interests at heart. Echoing the old woman and the swan in the first prologue at the beginning of the novel, mother Lindo Jong explains her feelings most poignantly: "I wanted everything for you to be better. I wanted you to have the best circumstances, the best character. I didn't want you to regret anything" (265). Because their own lives in China had been circumscribed by social and parental constraints that invariably led to pain, humiliation, and tragedy, the mothers all came to America to give their daughters a better life. However, daughters must first understand the real circumstances surrounding their mothers: how they arrived in their new country, how they married, how hard they tried to hold onto their Chinese roots. Once they have understood this, the daughters are better able to understand why they themselves are the way they are. Ultimately, this understanding will also lead them to finally appreciate their mothers.

M. MARIE BOOTH FOSTER ON DEVELOPING A VOICE, DEVELOPING AN IDENTITY

In *The Joy Luck Club* and *The Kitchen God's Wife*, Amy Tan uses stories from her own history and myth to explore the voices of mothers and daughters of Chinese ancestry. Each woman tells a story indicative of the uniqueness of her voice. Mary Field Belensky, in *Women's Ways of Knowing*, argues that voice is "more than an academic shorthand for a person's point of view . . . it is a metaphor that can apply to many aspects of women's experience and development. . . . Women repeatedly used the metaphor of voice to depict their intellectual and ethical development; . . . the development of a sense of voice, mind, and self were intricately intertwined" (18). In Tan's fiction, the daughters' sense of self is intricately linked to an ability to speak and be heard by their mothers. Similarly, the mothers experience growth as they broaden communication lines with their daughters. Tan's women are very much like the women Belensky portrays in *Women's Ways of Knowing*: "In describing their lives, women commonly talked about voice and silence: 'speaking up,' 'speaking out,' 'being silenced,' 'not being heard,' 'really listening,' 'really talking,' 'words as weapons,' 'feeling deaf and dumb,' 'having no words,' 'saying what you mean,' 'listening to be heard'" (18). Until Tan's women connect as mothers and daughters, they experience strong feelings of isolation, a sense of disenfranchisement and fragmentation. . . .

The Joy Luck Club and *The Kitchen God's Wife* are studies in balance—balancing hyphenation and the roles of daughter, wife, mother, sister, career woman. In achieving balance, voice is important: in order to achieve voice, hyphenated women must engage in self-exploration, recognition and appreciation of their culture(s), and they must know their histories. The quest for voice becomes an archetypal journey for all of the women. The mothers come to the United States and have to adapt to a new culture, to redefine voice and self. The daughters' journeys become rites of passage; before they can find voice or define self they must acknowledge the history and myth of their mothers—"her-stories" of life in China, passage to the United States, and assimilation. And each must come to grips with being her mother's daughter. . . .

Regardless of how much the daughters try to deny it, it is through their mothers that they find their voice, their mind, their selfhood. Voice finds its form in the process of interaction, even if that interaction is conflict. . . .

The mothers struggle to tell their daughters the consequences of not listening to them. The mother in the tale prefacing the section "Twenty-six Malignant Gates" tells her daughter not to ride her bike around the corner where she cannot see her because she will fall down and cry. The daughter questions how her mother knows, and she tells her that it is written in the book *Twenty-six Malignant Gates* that evil things can happen when a child goes outside the protection of the house. The daughter wants evidence, but her mother tells her that it is written in Chinese. When her mother does not tell her all twenty-six of the Malignant Gates, the girl runs out of the house and around the corner and falls, the consequence of not listening to her mother. Rebellion causes conflict. . . . June Woo and Waverly Jong seem to be daughters who thrive on the conflict that results from rebellion and sometimes even the need to win their mother's approval. June trudges off every day to piano lessons taught by an old man who is hard of hearing. Defying her mother, she learns very little, as she reveals at a piano recital to which her mother has invited all of her friends. June notes the blank look on her mother's face that says she has lost everything. Waverly wins at chess, which pleases her mother, but out of defiance she stops playing until she discovers that she really enjoyed her mother's approval. As an adult she wants her mother to approve of the man who will be her second husband; mother and daughter assume the positions of chess players.

Tan's mothers frequently preach that children are to make their mothers proud so that they can brag about them to other mothers. The mothers engage in fierce competition with each other. Suyuan Woo brags about her daughter even after June's poorly performed piano recital. All of the mothers find fault with their daughters, but this is something revealed to the daughters, not to the community.

Much as Lindo Jong credits herself with daughter Waverly's ability to play chess, she blames herself for Waverly's faults as a person and assumes failures in raising her daughter: "It is my fault she is this way—selfish. I wanted my children to have the best combination: American circumstances and Chinese character. How could I know these things do not mix?" (289). Waverly knows how American circumstances work, but Lindo can't teach her about Chinese character: "How to obey parents and listen to your mother's mind. How not to show your own thoughts, to put your feelings behind your face so you can take advantage of hidden opportunities. . . . Why Chinese thinking is best" (289). What she gets is a daughter who wants to be Chinese because it is fashionable, a daughter who likes to speak back and question what she says, and a daughter to whom promises mean nothing. Nonetheless, she is a daughter of whom Lindo is proud.

Lindo Jong is cunning, shrewd, resourceful; Waverly Jong is her mother's daughter. Waverly manages to irritate her mother when she resists parental guidance. . . . [She] is a strategist in getting her brother to teach her to play chess, in winning at chess, in gaining her mother's forgiveness when she is rude and getting her mother's acceptance of the man she plans to marry. Lindo proudly reminds Waverly that she has inherited her ability to win from her. . . .

Waverly is champion of the chess game, but she is no match for her mother in a life chess game. She knows her chances of winning in a contest against her mother, who taught her to be strong like the wind. Waverly learns during the "chess years" that her mother was a champion strategist. Though she is a tax attorney able to bully even the Internal Revenue Service, she fears the wrath of her mother if she is told to mind her business: "Well, I don't know if it's explicitly stated in the law, but you can't ever tell a Chinese mother to shut up. You could be charged as an accessory to your own murder" (191). What Waverly perceives as an impending battle for her mother's approval of her fiancé is nothing more than the opportunity for her mother and her to communicate with each other. She strategically plans to win her mother's approval of her fiancé, Rick, just as if she is playing a game of chess. She is afraid to tell her mother that they are going to be married because she is afraid that her mother will not approve. The conversation ends with her recognition that her mother also needs to be heard and with her mother's unstated approval of her fiancé. Waverly Jong recognizes her mother's strategies in their verbal jousts, but she also recognizes that, just like her, her mother is in search of something. What she sees is an old woman waiting to be invited into her daughter's life. Like the other mothers, Lindo views herself as standing outside her daughter's life—a most undesirable place. . . .

From the daughter with too much water, to the mother and daughter with too much wood, to the tiger ghosts and just plain ghosts, to the chess queens, Tan's women in *The Joy Luck Club* find themselves capable of forging their own identities, moving beyond passivity to assertiveness—speaking up. They are a piece of the portrait that represents Amy Tan's family history— her own story included; they are, in composite, her family's secrets and tragedies. Tan is unlike some Asian American writers who have had to try to piece together and sort out the meaning of the past from shreds of stories overheard or faded photographs. . . .

In exploring the problems of mother–daughter voices in relationships, Tan unveils some of the problems of biculturalism—of Chinese ancestry and American circumstances. She presents daughters who do not know their mothers' "importance" and thus cannot know their own;

most seem never to have been told or even cared to hear their mothers' history. Until they do, they can never achieve voice. They assimilate; they marry American men and put on American faces. They adapt. In the meantime, their mothers sit like Lady Sorrowfree on her altar, waiting to listen. The daughters' journeys to voice are completed only after they come to the altars of their Chinese mothers.

STEVEN P. SONDRUP ON THE MULTIPLE USES OF LANGUAGE IN *THE JOY LUCK CLUB*

The issue I wish to raise . . . is that of the status of the Chinese language in a narratological sense in *The Joy Luck Club*.[4] By definition the Chinese American novel—a specific species of the Asian American novel—is written in English, but Chinese, usually either Yue (or Cantonese as it is more typically known in the United States) or Mandarin, is part of the texture of the novel, a texture that conspicuously plays a role in the narrative strategy in some cases or in others is so smooth it almost vanishes. *The Joy Luck Club* is decidedly of the former type. . . .

The Joy Luck Club narrates the maturation of four second-generation Chinese women and their eventual bonding with their mothers, all of whom had left China in the hope of finding a better life. Each of these four mothers who played mah-jong together for decades tries in the course of many years to tell her daughter about her past and especially her relationship with her mother in a way in which the values of traditional China, the Chinese diaspora, and male Eurocentrism are engaged. The nature and dynamics of storytelling which create an alternative space and a different history distinct from the official accounts of war and political strife in China during the 1930s and 1940s are foregrounded and become one of the principle axes of the novel.

The linguistic competence of the major characters in the novel is clearly presented. The mothers are all native speakers of Mandarin and are thus a distinct minority in the

Chinese American community which is made up of about eighty-six per cent speakers of Cantonese (Ramsey 1987:98). This marginalization within a marginalized community, however, is an issue that is touched upon only in passing. The daughters grow up hearing varying amounts of Mandarin spoken at home and understand their mothers when they speak Mandarin but do not achieve any significant degree of oral fluency themselves. Notably, none can read Chinese, a fact which is a difficulty in that spoken Chinese is much more strongly linked to writing than Western languages are to their respective written forms. The attempt to clarify which meaning of a particular homophone is intended by reference to the appropriate character is incomprehensible and alien to the second generation. The daughters' inability to read Chinese characters, however, stresses the importance of the spoken language and immediate interpersonal relationships as opposed to depersonalized abstractions. The value of the intimacy of an oral tradition that strongly contrasts with the official and public tradition and in many ways subverts it is forcefully adduced. . . .

Some of the most obvious misunderstandings between the immigrant mothers and those around them have to do with their less than complete mastery of English. Language difficulties have long been part of the caricature of Chinese Americans in American popular culture and take place on many levels. Direct quotations of the mothers' speech are often unidiomatic in English but fully reveal the Chinese syntax lying just below the surface. After a heated description on the difference between Taiyuan and Taiwan, Lindo Jong triumphantly proclaims, 'Now you understand my meaning' (203). Although the intent is perfectly clear, the statement seems peculiar in English but can easily be recognized as a word for word translation of *xianzai ni mingbai wode yisi*. The phonological struggles with English in *The Joy Luck Club*, however, are often witty and provide a telling commentary on contemporary American culture. When Ying-ying St. Clair refers to her social security (the government mandated system of retirement payments) as 'so-so security' (275), the contemporary American will easily understand how such a misunderstanding on the phonetic level could take place but also that 'so-so' in the sense of mediocre and barely adequate is not an altogether inappropriate description of the current state of the system. On another occasion, Suyuan Woo misunderstands a vulgar insult directed toward her in a neighbourhood disagreement in a wonderfully ironic manner. Reporting on the verbal exchange, she says:

> 'And that man, he raise his hand like this, show me his ugly fist and call me worst Fukien landlady. I not from Fukien. Huuh! He know nothing!' she said satisfied she had put him in his place. (224)

Her inability or refusal to understand the single most vulgar and socially unacceptable word in American English is a misprision that rejects the common and base (albeit in the new culture), insists literally on social legitimacy, and reaffirms her insistence on things of only the best quality, the explicit theme of the chapter in which the exchange takes place but more generally the novel as a whole.

The misunderstanding, though, is doing something more. The reader who is also familiar with Chinese will recognize in the word *Fukien* not a standard place name but rather a variation of *Fujian*, that is, Fujian province. To interpret and make sense of her angry neighbour's vulgar appellation which she does not understand or refuses to understand in English requires recourse to Chinese and specifically a dialectical form. Although Suyuan Woo is not in fact from Fujian province, the interpretive process legitimizes Chinese, dialectical Chinese, and English in a complex referential system. This incident is but one example of the rich polyvalence resulting from the interplay of Chinese and English. . . .

This intersection of generations, cultures, and languages— both official and unsanctioned—constitutes a particularly rich signifying system and complex narrative architecture. One of the most arresting examples is the use of the Chinese word *bing*. It first occurs in the account of the childhood of Rose Hsu Jordan as the name of one of her four brothers: Matthew,

Mark, Luke, and Bing. Particularly in the context of a chapter that begins with a description of An-Mei Hsu's Christian faith, the appearance of the name Bing at the end of a list of the New Testament evangelists is particularly disarming. Neither Christian tradition nor mainstream American culture seems to offer any obvious explanation for this curious series of names. Seeking an explanation in terms of what could be a Chinese name is, moreover, problematic because no Chinese tone is marked so the precise reading and meaning is indeterminable. The range of possible meanings is broad. If one assumes the first tone, among the possibilities are: a soldier or a pawn; or ice, icicles, or frost. Assuming the third tone: bright, luminous; to grasp or to hold; or cakes, biscuits, or pastry. Assuming the fourth tone: sickness, disease, a fault or defect, or to be distressed about; together with, incorporate, merge, combine, united; even or equal; or to drive off, to expel, or to arrange. Although this array would not present itself in a Chinese text because each sense would be represented by a different character, this specially forged narrative language—part English, part Chinese, part standardized, part free invention, and part a hybrid combination—offers wide-ranging interpretive possibilities. The immediate narrative situation helps isolate some meanings that may be heuristically helpful. Bing is the youngest of four brothers. On a family excursion to the beach, he wanders off and is drowned in the ocean never to be seen again. In this context, the cluster of meanings associated with sickness, disease, defect and distress certainly suggest themselves. Bing's tragic death would certainly justify an epithet suggesting defect and distress. Although the information that one of the possible readings of Bing provides adds to the character and power of the situation, it does not go very far in accounting for his presence among Matthew, Mark, and Luke.

The word, however, appears in another context. When Waverly Jong becomes very angry with her mother's manipulation and condescending insults, she angrily goes to her parents' home. In a discussion that begins with Waverly's confusing Taiyuan, her mother's home, with Taiwan, her mother in exasperation explains that another name for Taiyuan is Bing and writes the character, though to no avail. The character, however, is very important. The ancient form has been interpreted as two people walking down the same road together, and indeed that chapter of the novel ends with an image of Waverly and Lindo Jong perhaps being able to set aside differences and walk the same path. Although in modern usage, *bing* means side by side, united, together, simultaneously, or merged (as with a small state and a large state), in classical Chinese, particularly during the Zhou dynasty, the more abstract sense of united, or two people or things closely associated, was more pronounced.[8] To the extent that the ancient conflation in one character of a city name and the sense of being side by side or united resonates in the chaotic cultural space of the narrated immigrant community, it enriches, strengthens, and broadens the force of the narrative.

What connection, though, is there between Bing as the alternative name of Taiyuan and the child named Bing who drowned? What interpretive strategy suggests that the two are anything but unrelated homophones? The only response is that the novel seems to invite the juxtaposition. In its portrayal of immigrant life on the fragmented margins of both Chinese and American culture, *The Joy Luck Club* is so conspicuously structured to disrupt any sense of the linear flow of time, conventional narrative practice, or normative language usage in order to make connections that otherwise would not be made that the tentative conjunction of the two seems almost required.

If the little boy's name is interpreted in terms of the idea of being side by side or united, his name is a deeply ironic and tragic contrast to his fate. Being held by the Coiled Dragon (138) beneath the sea, he is completely separated from his family and particularly his mother. The poignancy of the loss is staggering. What, though, of Bing's relationship to his brothers, Matthew, Mark, and Luke in the biblical framework these names suggest? The Apostle John, whose place Bing has taken in the catalogue of the evangelists, has a very rich tradition associated with him: the beloved Apostle, the Apostle who elected to remain on earth until the second coming of Jesus, and the Apostle who beheld the apocalyptic end of the earth and recorded his vision. The element of the Johanine tradition most relevant here, though, is the emphasis throughout his gospel and to a lesser degree in the epistles on unity, on the community of believers, and on the mystical union of the trinity.[9] What links Bing to the evangelist John is, thus, the theme of unity deriving on the one hand from a major theme in the Gospel of John and on the other from one of the earliest senses of the Chinese word *bing*. In the episode dealing with the boy named Bing, he represents the tragically ironic reversal of what his name suggests and, unlike the Apostle John, he is precisely the one who is not permitted to linger.

Chinese at the Joy Luck Club obviously fulfills all of the immediate expectations. It provides the effect of the real by creating the ambience and linguistic color expected in a Chinese immigrant community. It also serves as a reliable index of assimilation: the poorer the mastery of Chinese, the greater the assimilation into American society. But beyond these rather obvious and predictable roles, Chinese significantly enhances the narrative power of the novel. The disruption of its norms by the first generation of immigrants parallels their distortions of English as non-native speakers and creates an alternative narrative space and a special mode of discourse that challenges official conventions but is exactly what is required for the telling of their stories. A medium of communication arises in which the seemingly most disparate of elements can find common ground and walk together just as the novel as a whole can be seen to hinge on the arduous, alienating and almost life-threatening challenge of finding common ground on which different generations, different cultures, different hopes, as well as the self and the other, can meet and walk together.

Notes

4. For a general introduction to the issues centring on language and ethnicity, see Harald Haarmann, *Language in Ethnicity: A View of Basic Ecological Relations*.

8. For example, *Zheng zhong xing yin yi zhong he da zi dian* (Comprehensive Large Dictionary of Forms, Pronunciations, and

Definitions, 2nd revised edition) under the entry for *bing* quotes Lin Yi-guang in pointing out that in Zhou Dynasty bronze script the word signified two people standing side by side united as one. And Couvreur's *Dictionnaire classique de la langue chinoise* (1963) offers the straightforward definition: 'deux personnes ou deux choses associées ensemble, associer ensemble deux personnes ou deux choses.'

9. The point is nowhere clearer than in John 17: 21–3: 'Jesus prays, that they all may be one; as thou, Father, art in me, and I in thee, that they also may be one in us: that the world may believe that thou hast sent me. And the glory which thou gavest me I have give them; that they may be one, even as we are one: I in them, and thou in me, that they may be made perfect in one; and that the world may know that thou hast sent me, and hast loved them, as thou hast loved me.' The view represented in the *Anchor Bible Dictionary* (Doubleday 1992) is typical: 'Oneness is the key to proper interpretation of the gospel of John. The key to unity in John is christological unity, specifically the unity of the Son with the Father. Jesus is the one shepherd, the one who is the exclusive shepherd of God's people (10:16). In 10:30 the christological oneness is stated most clearly: I and the Father are one (4:752).'

PATRICIA L. HAMILTON ON THE INFLUENCE OF FENG SHUI IN THE NOVEL

A persistent thematic concern in Amy Tan's *The Joy Luck Club* is the quest for identity. Tan represents the discovery process as arduous and fraught with peril. Each of the eight main characters faces the task of defining herself in the midst of great personal loss or interpersonal conflict. . . . The mothers draw on a broad experiential base for their knowledge of American patterns of thought and behavior, but the daughters have only fragmentary, second-hand knowledge of China derived from their mothers' oral histories and from proverbs, traditions, and folktales.[1] Incomplete cultural knowledge impedes understanding on both sides, but it particularly inhibits the daughters from appreciating the delicate negotiations their mothers have performed to sustain their identities across two cultures.

Jing-mei, recalling that she talked to her mother Suyuan in English and that her mother answered back in Chinese, concludes that they "never really understood one another": "We translated each other's meanings and I seemed to hear less than what was said, while my mother heard more" (37). What is needed for any accurate translation of meanings is not only receptiveness and language proficiency but also the ability to supply implied or missing context. The daughters' inability to understand the cultural referents behind their mothers' words is nowhere more apparent than when the mothers are trying to inculcate traditional Chinese values and beliefs in their children. The mothers inherited from their families a centuries-old spiritual framework, which, combined with rigid social constraints regarding class and gender, made the world into an ordered place for them. Personal misfortune and the effects of war have tested the women's allegiance to traditional ideas, at times challenging them to violate convention in order to survive. But the very fact of their survival is in large measure attributable to their belief that people can affect their own destinies. In the face of crisis the mothers adhere to ancient Chinese practices by which they try to manipulate fate to their advantage. . . .

Ultimately, Tan endorses the mothers' traditional Chinese worldview because it offers the possibility of choice and action in a world where paralysis is frequently a threat. However, readers who are not specialists in Chinese cosmology share the same problematic relation to the text as the daughters do to their mothers' native culture: they cannot always accurately translate meanings where the context is implied but not stated. Bits of traditional lore crop up in nearly every story, but divorced from a broader cultural context, they are likely to be seen as mere brushstrokes of local color or authentic detail. Readers may be tempted to accept at face value the daughters' pronouncements that their mothers' beliefs are no more than superstitious nonsense. To ensure that readers do not hear less than what Tan is actually saying about the mothers' belief systems and their identities, references to Chinese cosmology in the text require explication and elaboration. . . .

[One] element of traditional belief in *The Joy Luck Club* is *feng shui*, or geomancy. The most opaque yet potentially the most important aspect of Chinese cosmology to Tan's exploration of identity, *feng shui* plays a pivotal role in Lena St. Clair's story "The Voice from the Wall," which chronicles her mother Ying-ying's gradual psychological breakdown and withdrawal from life. Ten-year-old Lena, having no knowledge of her mother's past, becomes convinced that her mother is crazy as she listens to Ying-ying rave after the death of her infant son. Even before Ying-ying loses her baby, however, her behavior appears to be erratic and compulsive. When the family moves to a new apartment, Ying-ying arranges and rearranges the furniture in an effort to put things in balance. Although Lena senses her mother is disturbed, she dismisses Ying-ying's explanations as "Chinese nonsense" (108). What Lena does not understand is that her mother is practicing the ancient Chinese art of *feng shui* (pronounced "fung shway"). Translated literally as "wind" and "water," *feng shui* is alluded to only once in the book as An-mei Hsu's balance of "the right amount of wind and water" (122). Although the term "*feng shui*" is never used overtly in conjunction with Ying-ying St. Clair, its tenets are fundamental to her worldview.

Stephen Skinner defines *feng shui* as "the art of living in harmony with the land, and deriving the greatest benefit, peace and prosperity from being in the right place at the right time" (4). The precepts of *feng shui* were systematized by two different schools in China over a thousand years ago. The Form School, or intuitive approach, was developed by Yang Yün-Sung (c. 840–888 A.D.). . . . Practitioners focus on the visible form of the landscape, especially the shapes of mountains and the direction of watercourses. The Compass School, or analytical approach, was developed by Wang Chih in the Sung dynasty (960 A.D.). . . . The analytic approach is concerned with directional orientation in conjunction with Chinese astrology. . . .

According to Susan Hornik, the beliefs encompassed by *feng shui* date back 3,000 years to the first practice of selecting auspicious sites for burial tombs in order to "bring good fortune to heirs" (73). As Skinner explains, "Ancestors are linked with the site of their tombs. As they also have a direct effect on the lives of their descendants, it follows logically that if their tombs are located favourably on the site of a strong concentration of earth energy or *ch'i*, not only will they be happy but they will also derive the power to aid their descendants, from the accumulated *ch'i* of the site" (11). By the Han dynasty (206 B.C.), the use of *feng shui* was extended to the selection of dwellings for the living (Hornik 73). The basic idea is to attract and channel *ch'i*, or beneficial energy, and "accumulate it without allowing it to go stagnant" (Skinner 21). Since *ch'i* encourages growth and prosperity, a wise person will consider how to manipulate it to best effect through *feng shui*, the study of placement with respect to both natural and man-made environments. . . . Whereas the course of the stars and planets is fixed, the earthly environment can be altered by human intervention through *feng shui*. The practice of *feng shui* offers yet another variation of the belief that people have the power to affect their destiny.

Thus Ying-ying St. Clair's seemingly idiosyncratic actions and their nonsensical explanations in "The Voice from the Wall" are grounded in a coherent system of beliefs and practices concerned with balancing the environment. Since Ying-ying feels her surroundings are out of balance, she does everything she can to correct them. For instance, she moves "a large round mirror from the wall facing the front door to a wall by the sofa" (108). *Ch'i* is believed to enter a dwelling through the front door, but a mirror hung opposite the entrance may deflect it back outside again. Mirrors require careful placement so as to encourage the flow of *ch'i* around a room. Furniture, too, must be positioned according to guidelines that allow beneficial currents of *ch'i* to circulate without stagnating. . . .

In light of the bad *feng shui* of the apartment, Ying-ying's unhappiness with it is logical. Once she finishes altering the living room, she rearranges Lena's bedroom. The immediate effect of the new configuration is that "the nighttime life" of Lena's imagination changes (109). With her bed against the wall, she begins to listen to the private world of the family next door and to use what she hears as a basis for comparison with her own family. . . .

The burden of guilt Ying-ying carries over an abortion from her first marriage is the root of her disturbed mental state during her pregnancy. Her bumping into table edges may even be a form of self-punishment. In any case, whether she has subconsciously tried to harm the fetus or has merely failed to fend off disaster through the use of *feng shui*, in blaming herself for the baby's death Ying-ying is clearly wrestling with her responsibility for the death of her first son. In her mind the two events are connected: "I knew he [the baby] could see everything inside me. How I had given no thought to killing my other son! How I had given no thought to having this baby" (112). Instead of finding any resolution after the baby dies, Ying-ying becomes increasingly withdrawn. She cries unaccountably in the middle of cooking dinner and frequently retreats to her bed to "rest."

The presence of *feng shui* in the story suggests that however displaced, demoralized, and severely depressed Ying-ying may be, she is not "crazy," as Lena fears. Ying-ying's compulsion to rearrange furniture does not presage a psychotic break with reality but rather signals that, transplanted to a foreign country where she must function according to new rules and expectations, Ying-ying relies on familiar practices such as *feng shui* and astrology to interpret and order the world around her, especially when that world is in crisis. Lena, of course, is locked into a ten-year-old's perspective and an American frame of reference. She shares Jing-mei Woo's problem of being able to understand her mother's Chinese words but not their meanings. Whereas Clifford St. Clair's usual practice of "putting words" in his wife's mouth stems from his knowing "only a few canned Chinese expressions" (106), Lena's faulty translation of her mother's distracted speech after the baby dies reflects a lack of sufficient personal and cultural knowledge to make sense of Ying-ying's references to guilt. . . .

Unlike her mother, Lena has no consistent belief system of her own. She inherits Ying-ying's ability to see bad things before they happen but does not possess the power to anticipate good things, which suggests that Lena has merely internalized "the unspoken terrors" that plague Ying-ying (103). According to Philip Langdon, "second- or third-generation Chinese-Americans are much less likely to embrace *feng shui* than are those who were born in Asia" (148). Not only is Lena a second-generation Chinese-American, she is half Caucasian, which makes her Chinese heritage even more remote. Nonetheless, Lena is profoundly affected by Ying-ying's way of perceiving the world. As a child Lena is obsessed with knowing the worst possible thing that can happen, but unlike her mother, she has no sense of being able to manipulate fate. Thus, she is terrified when she cannot stop what she supposes to be the nightly "killing" of the girl next door, which she hears through her bedroom wall. Only after Lena realizes that she has been wrong about the neighbor family does she find ways to change the "bad things" in her mind.

Note

1. For a discussion of existential unrepeatability and the role of memory in *The Joy Luck Club*, see Ben Xu, "Memory and the Ethnic Self: Reading Amy Tan's *The Joy Luck Club*," *MELUS* 19.1 (1994): 3–18. An interesting treatment of language, storytelling, and maternal subjectivity in Tan's novel can be found in Marina Heung, "Daughter-Text/Mother-Text: Matrilineage in Amy Tan's *Joy Luck Club*," *Feminist Studies* 19.3 (1993): 597–616.

WENDY HO ON A JOY LUCK CLUB FATHER

In *The Joy Luck Club*, Amy Tan tells father–daughter stories too. As young women in China, Joy Luck mothers certainly speak of their oppressive relationships with Chinese males like Wu Tsing and Tyan Yu (Lindo's boy-husband). But despite their bad experiences, three of the Joy Luck mothers love and marry Chinese men who can live with clever, practical, and independent-minded women. For example, An-mei Hsu and Lindo meet each other in a fortune cookie factory and become friends. In immigrant women's extended social and political networks, women find support, jobs, and husbands. An-mei and her husband George set Lindo up on a blind date with a telephone man named Tin Jong. Both Tin and Lindo overcome their initial ethnic and linguistic differences (Cantonese and Mandarin) and woo each other through a new language, English. They have a delightful, practical courtship—not the silly story Waverly tells. Rather than enduring an arranged marriage, the feisty, pragmatic Lindo chooses the man she will marry this time around, and this makes a difference in her life. She tells Waverly not only to be proud of her mother's Sun clan but also of her father's Jong clan.

The Joy Luck mothers also toil beside their husbands and teach their children the importance of surviving and maintaining cultural traditions as well as hybrid culture in the minefields of Anglo-American society. The couples travel, play mah jong and socialize together, and learn to pool their resources and invest for their retirement together. This extended social network of husbands and wives extends support to each other's children. The men respect the work of their wives in the care of their children. Resituated in the United States, these couples both enact more hybrid gendered identities in their relationships and continue a social understanding of self-in-community that is, in part, derived from their Chinese world view. Rather than arranged marriages, most of the Joy Luck mothers find more companionate, fluid marriages with Chinese men. Furthermore, the mothers do not tell their daughters never to marry Chinese men; rather, they tell their daughters to be strong and independent first and to affiliate with partners who will love and respect them in their own right.

Though not made central in Tan's recovery of mother–daughter stories, Chinese American fathers are represented in *The Joy Luck Club* as dignified, beloved, and respected presences in the lives of the Joy Luck daughters. Canning Woo, June's father, for example, asks his daughter to take her deceased mother's place in the circle of Joy Luck "aunts." June loves the father who takes care of her and who honors his wife's story of struggle. Canning keeps her memory alive in the extended family's archives, as a subversive form of ancestor worship that does honor to his deceased wife as well as to himself. Through his nurture and respect for mother and daughter, he reveals aspects of Suyuan's stories that will bring June to a closer understanding of her mother. He lovingly tells his wife's story to his family in China and to his daughter. And in the telling, he does not skip the *emotional* details—the inner turmoil of her struggle.

Suyuan and Canning meet in a hospital in Chungking during the revolutionary war years in China. She is distraught and suicidal, suffering guilt in abandoning her twin daughters, and is sick with dysentery. She loses her soldier husband in the war. Canning Woo nurses Suyuan back to health through these chaotic and nomadic war years in China. She marries him and they search for her children in Shanghai; and after a long period of wandering together through China and Hong Kong, they both make their way to the United States in 1949. Canning Woo is involved in the nurturing of his wife and family as part of his understanding of meaningful manhood. In the final story, it is he who accompanies June to China in order to reunite her with extended family and with his stepdaughters.

Tan, therefore, honors a father's role in building family, community, and solidarity not just in public or work sites, but also at the homeplace. Canning Woo does not easily fit into Anglo-American or Asian American cultural nationalist notions of male-warrior identities. He does not rampage like a stereotyped heartless Confucian patriarch or a kung-fu fighter through his daughter's life or his family's. He is also not represented as an effeminate or castrated wimp. Instead, Canning Woo models a construction of manhood that is, I believe, emotionally and socially responsible and nurturant. It is a more democratic and permeable notion of Chinese American manhood that does not need to dissociate from women or display a traditional form of masculinity that constantly asserts and reenacts its repudiation of femininity (see Kimmel 1996, 318).

Furthermore, what needs to be more profoundly healed is not the father wound but the *mother* wound in men (ibid.). That is, the part of the male self that denies or represses emotion, which masks vulnerability, fear, and depression; but which needs to love and be loved, and to nurture and be nurtured, as part of the *human condition*. In privileging and reproducing restrictive and debilitating patriarchal binary systems, it seems that some men have "abandoned precisely those emotional skills that were most needed if women were to achieve equality: nurture, sensitivity, emotional responsiveness" (ibid.). Sheila Ruth makes a good point that "the idea that one who is capable of emotion and sensitivity is incapable of discipline and rational [or intellectual] judgement is absurd. . . . It bespeaks no *undesirable* softness (again, the martial belief that 'softness' is contemptible), no lack of intellect or strength" (Ruth 1990, 215).

Cultural nationalists and critics rarely refer to these men's stories in the work of Tan or Kingston in articulating more expansive, fluid personal and political identities. They do not refer to the tradition of Asian American feminist writing that explores the nature of heroism and the nature of male suffering, anger, and violence in a racist, sexist world, and that acknowledges the contributions of Chinese American men to their families and communities. In making only certain forms of manhood visible or acceptable, masculinity and racialized discourses impose a debilitating *invisibility* to this rich area of men's (and women's) experiences. From their restricted militaristic rhetorical stance, they cannot see these potentially alternative and resisting men's stories as heroic, but only as "emasculating" or "feminizing." As Judith Newton states, more work needs to be done at "the site of investigating masculinity," work that links the "economic and political with the familial and personal, the public with the private" (Newton 1994, 575). Such links are vital to explore if women and men are to build towards more liberating practices in a society.

PATRICIA P. CHU ON BALANCING THE NOVEL'S STRENGTHS AND WEAKNESSES

[*The Joy Luck Club*] continues the Asian American exploration of the problem of defining Asian American difference within a broader claim of commonality with other Americans. On what terms, the text seems to ask, can we recognize these mothers as American in their core values yet still retaining values that are Chinese? Most importantly, which values, common to subjects in both cultures, transcend the "East is not West" fallacy?

Tan's answer to this problem draws upon feminist thinking to invoke the struggle for personal agency—control of the decisions that define one's life—as common to girls and young women in both China and America. In the end, I think Tan's difficulty is that she bases her understanding of female agency on her experiences as a middle-class American in a postfeminist era without being fully aware of how privileged this position is. In the stories of two yuppie daughters (Lena and Rose), the key to regaining self-respect, claiming better treatment from males, and beginning a new life is simple self-assertiveness. Thus, Rose Hsu Jordan, whose passive dependence on her husband has extinguished his interest in her, learns that she can force him to make a generous divorce settlement, and even scare him, merely by deciding to become self-assertive again. "The power of my words was that strong," she concludes (196). Rose's passivity, explained as both an individual psychic deficiency and a symptom of feminine conditioning, vanishes so quickly that one wonders why she didn't clear it up sooner. Although somewhat simplistic, such solutions are appropriate for these characters because, for women of their class and era, other elements necessary for their "liberation" from debilitating marriages are available to them: education, the possibility of supporting themselves, family support, legal rights, and a well-established public ideology of women's equality. The novel doesn't really need to acknowledge this environment as the product of the American women's movement because this social context is familiar to American readers. On the other hand, because the novel lacks historical self-consciousness about the enabling conditions for female self-assertion in America, it naively universalizes its lessons about self-empowerment, disregarding the more serious obstacles to autonomy faced by Chinese women, as we shall see by examining the circumstances for self-empowerment described in Lindo Jong's story, "The

Red Candle." Whereas a sense of self-worth may be a necessary condition for women's survival or liberation in China, it isn't a sufficient guarantee of either unless other conditions also prevail. Thus, the novel's understanding of female agency, and its efforts to compare Chinese and American female oppression, are dependent on simplistic analogies between two groups of women whose differing social conditions aren't fully clarified by the book's optimistic treatment.

* * *

Before assessing what is marginalized by Tan's narrative method, it's only fair to acknowledge what is achieved: clear plots in which heroic young women, undergoing trials by ordeal, arrive at epiphanies of character that carry them through their ordeals and, implicitly or explicitly, to America. Lindo Jong's story, "The Red Candle," is the most compact and winsome version of this type of story. It goes like this: she is betrothed at age two to marry into a rich family, the Huangs. When she is twelve, her peasant family is ruined by river floods. They have to move far away but leave her to be brought up by the Huangs. Before leaving, her mother insists that Lindo uphold the family honor by devoting her life to fulfilling the family's marriage contract. Lindo's natal family then disappears completely from her life. Although the Huangs treat her more like a servant than a family member, Lindo remains and does her best to please them, both because of her mother's wishes and because there is no alternative. After her marriage at sixteen, she's relieved to find that her husband, who's slightly younger, avoids touching her. This means she can sleep in peace but can't produce the required male heir despite the threats and confinement imposed by Huang Taitai, her mother-in-law. Having recognized that a servant girl whom she likes is concealing an illegitimate pregnancy, Lindo uses bogus supernatural tokens to persuade Huang Taitai that the family will be cursed by her continued presence and blessed if they trade her in for the servant, whose pregnancy the Huangs have not yet noticed. The Huangs accordingly bribe Lindo to accept a quiet divorce and leave town; they marry their son to the pregnant servant and thereby (it's implied) get their heir (so to speak). Lindo escapes with honor and a nest egg, to Beijing and thence to America, rescues the servant from ruin, and saves the Huangs from patrilineal extinction in the process.

The features of Lindo's story that recur, with variations, in those of her friends are these: a young girl or young woman is forced to face extreme adversity or injustice, either alone or with the support of a powerless mother. Aside from her mother, the heroine has no friends or allies either within or beyond the family circle. The heroine's initial condition of hopeless victimization is represented as emblematic of the condition of all women in China, which is basically seen as a static feudal society. Each heroine, however, discovers within herself a reservoir of self-esteem, resourcefulness, and dissatisfaction with her prescribed low status, and each finds a way to escape her entrapment and come to America.

These positive qualities, which appear in each mother's story at some point, are most clearly defined in the case of Lindo. The text portrays her in-laws, both son and mother, as a self-absorbed pair who see her as a combination of servant, breeding stock, and chattel (indeed, many traditional Chinese proverbs compare the taking of a wife to the purchase of livestock). But Lindo survives and ultimately escapes the marriage because of outstanding personal qualities, which are depicted as intrinsic to her and are, in terms of the social milieu depicted, inexplicable. These qualities, the greatest of which is courage, define Lindo; they are also, I would argue, definitive within this text of the immigrant sensibility—that which marks the Chinese mothers as unfit for their old world milieu and destined to become Americans. In the Chinese scenes, almost everyone else accepts the status quo and criticizes those who don't. Only the young protagonists have a version of "Hamlet's dis-ease": they recognize that the world is out of joint. But whereas Hamlet, as a prince, feels "born to set it right," these young women are placed in a fictional Chinese world where both individual justice and systemic social change seem impossible. They cannot set things right; they can only seek survival, then freedom, for themselves. Therefore, they must come to America.

The sign of this Americanizing discontent is usually a scene in which the young woman rallies her spirits and determines to take charge of her future. In Lindo's story, the possibility of controlling her own fate comes to her as an epiphany of psychological autonomy, which takes place, appropriately enough, before a mirror. In Lindo's life, the Fen River represents the inevitability of fate; it's a Fen River flood that ruins her peasant family, forcing them to leave town and abandon her to the Huangs' tender mercies. Four years later, as she considers casting herself into the river to avoid her wedding—a gesture combining defiance with defeat—she's distracted and heartened by the power of the wind, which exerts terrific force on both the river and the humans in her view. Her formative scene of self-recognition follows: "I wiped my eyes and looked in the mirror. I was surprised at what I saw. I had on a beautiful red dress, but what I saw was even more valuable. I was strong. I was pure. I had genuine thoughts inside that no one could see, that no one could ever take away from me. I was like the wind" (58). Here Lindo grants herself the subjectivity no one else has offered her. In the story, she has been conditioned all her life to deny her desires, imagination, and will, a schooling the novel identifies with Chinese female experience. Now she alone recognizes and values her own interiority, the intelligence that both parents and in-laws have systematically sought to stifle lest it foster discontent and rebellion. Strikingly, intelligence is linked by Lindo with a new perception of her sexuality as something strong and good that she herself commands. Because Lindo's intelligence and the mental freedom it adds to her life are unrecognized by those around her, it is an invaluable weapon in her struggle for survival and freedom. This invisible source of strength, as well as the real freedom she seeks, is henceforth linked with the wind, which has the power to manipulate the river of fate and the power to carry her to America. . . .

The "just say yes" fable of self-determination, which can readily be recognized by American readers as simplistic but not entirely removed from reality for the middle-class American daughters, is more problematic in a story like Lindo's because Tan cannot assume an equivalent understanding of the Chinese social context in her American readership, nor does she provide quite enough context in this story or elsewhere in the novel. As a result, Tan's novel tends to give the impression that Lindo Jong, An-mei Hsu, and to a lesser extent Ying-ying St. Clair passed readily from a very traditional Confucian society into the American middle class with little mention of such mediating forces as the questioning of traditional family structures by Chinese reformers, feminist movements within China, the influence of Western education and ideas on Chinese elites, and the struggles of Chinese on many levels—including the level of domestic social structures—to modernize their country.[11] Such forces, which are reduced to the level of rumor in a story like "The Red Candle," would help prepare Chinese women and men of the educated classes for immigration to America and a relatively easy transition into the professional classes here, in contrast to others, who, coming to the United States without English or readily negotiable professional credentials, connections, or capital, would probably enter the ranks of the working poor.[12] In Tan's novel, the characterization of the fourth mother, Suyuan Woo, is most free of the problem of improbable discontinuities in class identity. Since she was trained as a nurse and married to two professional men (a Kuomintang officer and then a journalist, June's father) in China, it's easier to imagine Suyuan picking up English and sending her children to college. What is present in the American stories, but absent from most of the Chinese ones, is the middle term identified by Rey Chow, the Chinese woman as a modern subject, and what that subject represents, the vision of early-twentieth-century China as a country in which modern and traditional elements coexist, a country that, like the United States, is constantly changing. . . .

If we relied on this novel, Lindo's reliance on empirical observation rather than conventional class or moral prejudices would seem to set her apart from almost everyone else in China—or at least from everyone else in "The Red Candle."

In addition, her practice of judging people by their conduct rather than their class status might be considered in the light of arguments that the very idea of an "inner self" distinguishable from one's outer social status is arguably a Western one. Lindo's empowering emphasis on her mental life—her "interiority"—is certainly not without Chinese literary precedent, but it also aligns her with Western fictional heroines whose mental purity transcends the limits or mortifications of their flesh.[14] Finally, she seems to be the one disbeliever in a community where everyone else takes the authority and supernatural power of dead ancestors literally. If the Chinese people around her are really so homogeneous in their thinking, how does Lindo, an isolated girl confined to these two households, arrive at a mind set so different, so seemingly Western?

When we next see young Lindo, she's in Beijing, copying English words and planning to enter the United States as a college student (of theology, no less). Arriving in America, she amuses herself with jokes about the signs in Chinatown, gets a job in a fortune cookie factory, and uses night school English classes to woo her future husband. Given the Huangs' feudal approach to female education, when did she learn to read Chinese and manage money? How did she learn of America, much less decide to come here? Once here, how does she jump from a cookie assembly line into the middle class? Glossed over are the obstacles to legal entry, and physical and social mobility, faced by most working-class immigrants. Instead, Lindo's lighthearted initiation into America seems more like that of an exchange student with a work-study job.

Such questions, however, beg a more fundamental one: how could Lindo have survived in China after she left the Huangs? Her own mother had preemptively refused to shelter her, and everyone in the village would have known she was the Huangs' daughter-in-law. Even had she found a way to reach the city, who would have sheltered, fed, or hired an unknown young woman from the provinces with no references? The absence of social support for runaway or castaway women is to become a central concern, and a central explanation for wife abuse, in Tan's next novel (*The Kitchen God's Wife*); in *Joy Luck* that absence implicitly explains the high tolerance for domestic abuse of Lindo, An-mei, and Ying-ying. It doesn't, however, explain how Lindo survived the sudden independence for which she had never been prepared.

In Lindo's case, Tan simply attributes an educated, arguably American, consciousness to her character. This serves the optimism of the immigration plot well, because it overstates the possibility of upward mobility in the United States. It serves the task of portraying actual immigrants' experiences less well, however, for it understates the working-class immigrant's struggle to survive (particularly when language barriers and race-based obstacles come into play) as well as the foreign student's loneliness, cultural isolation, and financial anxiety. Admittedly, the class disparity between the narrator's mind and her ostensible background is greatest in Lindo's narratives, and the resulting overstatement of the character's freedom and agency, while historically implausible, is part of the book's charm. Given the difficulty of Tan's cross-cultural project, it seems better that she has chosen to overstate rather than understate Lindo's intelligence and agency. It is merely regrettable that "The Red Candle" depends on portraying other Chinese characters as self-absorbed, maliciously exploitative, and unthinking in their adherence to the letter, but not the spirit, of their traditional religious beliefs.

Notes

11. Historian Jonathan Spence argues in *The Search for Modern China* (New York: Norton, 1990) that with the abdication of the last Ching emperor in 1912 the following decades of social and political upheaval were also characterized by an ongoing search for new ideas about how to govern China, with Western liberal democracies and the Russian socialist system emerging as the most significant foreign models. Significant histories of feminist movements in China, which may counter the notion of classical China as socially unchanged for the first five decades of this century, are offered by Elisabeth Croll, *Feminism and Socialism in China* (London: Routledge, 1978); Kazuko Ono, *Chinese Women in a Century of Revolution, 1850–1950*, trans. Kathryn Bernhardt et al., ed. Joshua A. Fogel (1978; Stanford: Stanford UP, 1989); and Kay Ann Johnson, *Women, the Family, and Peasant Revolution in China* (Chicago: UP of Chicago, 1983). Such

histories, combined with the novel about to be discussed, confirm Tan's sense that Chinese women had few means of resisting the sex-gender system characterized by arranged marriages, but they also provide a more complex and varied sense of how the Chinese inhabited this system and how it could continue despite being a source of misery for so many.

12. On the experiences of Chinese women immigrants in America, see Judy Yung, *Unbound Feet: A Social History of Chinese Women in San Francisco* (Berkeley: U of California P, 1995).

14. Concepts of the self vary within cultures, but a useful starting point might be Alan Roland's discussion of the Western philosophical roots of psychoanalytic concepts of self, as contrasted with May Tung's account of Chinese concepts of the self. See Alan Roland, "How Universal Is The Psychoanalytic Self?" (3–21, esp. 3–13), and May Tung, "Insight-Oriented Therapy and the Chinese Patient" (175–86), both in Alan Roland, *Cultural Pluralism and Psychoanalysis: The Asian and North American Experience* (New York: Routledge, 1996).

PETER X. FENG ON TAKING *THE JOY LUCK CLUB* FROM NOVEL TO FILM

[In] deploying multiple narratives about Chinese and Chinese American women, *The Joy Luck Club* invokes many . . . discourses about representation, representativeness, and women's negotiation of migration between Asian and U.S. patriarchies. *The Joy Luck Club* features multiple narrators who invoke folk sayings to make sense of their experiences. . . .

[S]creenwriter Ronald Bass suggested . . . taking the novel's various short stories and reorganizing them. Amy Tan's best-selling novel[10] consists of four groupings of four short stories, with each section introduced by an italicized story written in pseudo-mythic style (characters are not named but called "the mother" and "the daughter"). The enunciative present of the novel takes place after the death of Suyuan Woo, the founder of the club; her stories are narrated by her daughter June.[11] Otherwise, the first group of stories is narrated by four Chinese immigrant women and emphasizes their childhood; the second group is narrated by their Chinese American daughters, who tell generally comic stories of their own childhood; the third features the daughters narrating tales of their adulthood, mostly comic stories about their romantic relationships; and the final section returns us to the mothers, who tell mostly tragic tales from their adult years. In their screenplay, Bass and Tan reshuffle the stories, taking the four stories narrated by Lindo and Waverly and grouping them together. They also integrated two of the italicized stories (attributing them to different characters) and invented a party where the seven surviving women mingle as a framing narrative.

The press kit for *The Joy Luck Club* emphasizes—and most articles about the film faithfully report—that Bass agreed to work on the screenplay on the condition that all sixteen stories in Tan's novel were retained in the film, and indeed early drafts of the screenplay do feature elements from all sixteen stories. This plan was abandoned soon after producer Patrick Markey (representing Disney's Hollywood Pictures division) came aboard and cut two of the stories—"The Moon Lady" and "Half and Half"—because, taking place on a lake and at the beach, they would have been extremely expensive and time-consuming to shoot (Hajari, 1993). Furthermore, for unstated reasons, only a fragment of the story "The Voice from the Wall" was retained, with the result that the Ying Ying–Lena storyline was severely compromised.[12] The artistic success of the film's narrative structure can be debated, yet the film generally handles the complexity of its shifting point-of-view structure with aplomb. The screenplay makes canny use of flashbacks, falsely cueing the audience that we are returning to the enunciative present of the party in order to facilitate the narrative shifts from the mothers to the daughters. For example, Lindo's tale of her childhood betrothal is motivated by an interior monologue. When the story ends, we return not to the party but to the recent past; this return is facilitated by a close-up of Lindo staring abstractly ahead, echoing the beginning of the flashback. After shifting to Waverly's story—within which Lindo narrates a story (this time motivated by Waverly's presence as interlocutor)—we return to Lindo at the party after much time has elapsed, again lost in a reverie. Lindo smiles as if she had been replaying a cherished moment with her daughter in her mind. If the entire preceding sequence represents Lindo's memory, how are we to account for Waverly's narration in the midst of Lindo's story? *The Joy Luck Club* presents many narrative conundrums like this one, but these moments pass by barely noticed due to the forward progress of the narrative. . . . *The Joy Luck Club* attempts to disguise these shifts, for, generally speaking, commercial cinema prefers not to draw attention to its enunciative techniques.

Identifying with *The Joy Luck Club*

An article that appeared in the *New York Times* the Sunday before its New York opening called attention to another narrative challenge for *The Joy Luck Club*: its large cast. "It is in fact difficult to assemble a large cast in which one character is not mistaken for another. The conventional solution is to pepper a cast with blonds, redheads and brunettes and different ethnic types. But the 'Joy Luck Club' does not have that liberty."[13] Faced with casting over fifty female roles (in two languages, English and Mandarin)—a task made more difficult by the fact that in some cases three actors of different ages would portray the same character at different stages in her life, not to mention the aspiration that mothers and daughters would bear some resemblance—Wayne Wang devised two rules when casting the film:

> First, no Caucasians would play roles written for Asians. "During the 'Miss Saigon' controversy," he said, "there were a lot of people who said, 'Talent is talent, and anybody can play any character with makeup.' But it never happens that an Asian actress can go out for a major Caucasian role and get it. Until that day comes, there is no equity, so it was important to me that these roles all go to Asians."
>
> Rule two was that actresses of various Asian backgrounds would be considered for specifically Chinese roles. "Because there are so few good roles for Asians, I didn't want to eliminate Japanese or Vietnamese or

Koreans," Mr. Wang explained. "The important thing was that they felt right for the role and would fit into the ensemble." (Avins, 1993, 2:14)

Wang's argument, as presented by the *Times*, is based purely on equity. He never says that a non-Asian actor cannot play an Asian role, only that such casting denies opportunities to Asian actors. However, by formulating the argument this way, Wang sidesteps the implications of casting non-Chinese in *The Joy Luck Club*; for example, when non-Asian filmmakers cast Rosalind Chao as a Korean on *M*A*S*H* or as a Japanese on *Star Trek: The Next Generation*, many Asian Americans are displeased. Wang goes on to argue that there are other aspects of performance that might affect ethnic realism—for example, he admits that an actress was not cast because her speech rhythms were more Japanese than Chinese—conceding that realism is the ultimate deciding factor but leaving open the question of who defines realism.[14] After all, did Wang foresee the complaints of some Mandarin speakers that all the Chinese characters in *The Joy Luck Club* spoke with Beijing accents?[15]

These and other discourses speak to the appropriateness and ability of the various actors cast in *The Joy Luck Club*. Promotional materials for narrative films often stress affinities between actor and character, laying claim to performative authenticity. For example, *Parade Magazine* reported that Ming-Na Wen brought her mother with her when she shot scenes in Shanghai ("A Mother and Daughter," 1993), and in the *New York Times* Wen described her first encounter with the novel: "For the first time, I felt I was reading something that was completely talking to me" (Avins, 1993, 2:14).[16] It is commonly reported that the narratives of ethnic "cross-over" films resonate with ethnic actors in a way that mainstream projects do not. By mentioning the amateur actors who attended open casting calls for the film, publicity for *The Joy Luck Club* lays claim both to the authenticity of these narrative representations and to their scarcity in the cinematic marketplace, simultaneously affirming that the narrative is original (insofar as Chinese American women's experiences have been marginalized by mainstream film) and commonplace (in telling a story that all Chinese American women know).[17] In the film's press kit, casting director Heidi Levitt states, "Every woman who came in had a story, whether it was about a sister, aunt or grandmother, that reflected these characters," and San Francisco casting director Robin Gurland commented, "When I initially read the book and then the screenplay, I thought that the characters' tragic lives were unique.... If anything the stories in the novel were minimized compared to the ones I heard from the women who auditioned."[18] Indeed, even the story's central narrative is attested to: in an interview, Wang referred to an extra who, overhearing the dialogue in the film's final scene, reported that she had left her baby during the war (Tibbetts, 1994, 5).[19] Furthermore, actor Kieu Chinh reported that abandoning the babies reminded her of leaving her father behind when she left North Vietnam. (According to Baker [1993], Wang encouraged Chinh to perform this scene in Vietnamese if it allowed her to draw on her experiences.)

The notion of auditors identifying with the stories they are told is alluded to in the film, when Rose tells her husband, "I died sixty years ago ... for my daughter's sake." Rose's identification with her grandmother seems less bizarre in an early draft of the screenplay, where the writers suggest that the same actor should be cast as the adult Rose and as her own grandmother in the stories related by Rose's mother, An-mei.[20] This story is based on the life of Tan's own grandmother, named Jing-mei (Tan, 1991a), a name that Tan gave to *Joy Luck Club*'s central character, Jing-mei Woo (also known as June). Like June/Jing-mei, Tan has both an English and a Chinese name: Amy and An-mei. Many critics have assumed that June is patterned after Tan (e.g., Tseo, 1996), in part because June's stories draw from Tan's experiences with the piano and working as a business writer.[21] Thus, readers familiar with the biography of Amy Tan can interpret her as June, Rose's mother An-mei (who shares Tan's Chinese name), and Rose (whose grandmother is based on Tan's grandmother).[22] Perhaps this is what Tan meant when she said, "All Chinese people are family to one another in some unexplainable way" (1989b, 302).

If I find assertions about the authenticity of the film (its connection to "real women's experiences") problematic, it is because they echo an assertion in the narrative itself: that daughters *can* go home again, returning to the motherland and indeed to unity with their mothers.[23] Following a dinner party where the Woo family hosts the Jongs, June comes to realize that her anger with her mother results from misunderstanding her mother's words. Suyuan had stated that Waverly and June had differing styles, which June interpreted to mean that Waverly was more stylish; in the kitchen, Suyuan makes clear that she means that June is morally superior to Waverly. Suyuan caps off this scene by telling her daughter "I *see you*," meaning she sees who June really is. When mother and daughter embrace, it is as if June is able to return from the realm of the Lacanian symbolic to that of the imaginary, where visual apprehension (being seen) supplies a truth that cannot be achieved by language (due to verbal misunderstanding).[24] *The Joy Luck Club* enacts a fantasy of reconciliation and reunification, and this fantasy is echoed whenever the film's promotion asserts an identity between actor and character.

There remains, however, one identification that does not deny historical rupture. Tamlyn Tomita reveals her keen awareness of her position in Hollywood when she is quoted in the film's press kit: "Ming-Na, Lauren, Rosalind and I often vie for the same projects because we're all Asian women of the same age range. . . . And Lisa, Kieu, Tsai and France are the women we grew up watching, they were our role models in the industry. To bring us all together and to hear each other's stories about surviving in the industry—those are secrets being passed between us." By mentoring the actors who play their daughters, *The Joy Luck Club*'s veteran actors become metaphoric mothers. It is, of course, a sign of commercial cinema's recuperative power that an anecdote about the limited roles Hollywood offers Asian American women is deployed to promote a movie coproduced by Walt Disney and Oliver Stone.

Although many of the promotional discourses for *The Joy Luck Club* called attention to the film's production, these narratives did not emphasize the film as a mediation but its continuity with Tan's novel and with the experiences of Asian American women (the sole exception being Tomita's commentary, which pointed not just to the material circumstances governing the production of *The Joy Luck Club* but indeed to the structure of the mainstream film industry generally). These discourses of continuity were in keeping with *The Joy Luck Club*'s fantasy of cross-generational reconciliation, of unity across historical discontinuity; in short, the affirmation of the movie as an effective and accurate translation of the book is part and parcel of the story's governing logic of reunion.

Notes

10. By September 1993, when the film opened, Tan's debut novel had sold over two million copies and been translated into twenty-three languages; it stayed on the *New York Times*'s best-seller list for a year and a half (Hajari, 1993). For an account of the roles that Tan's agent, editors, and publishers played in developing and promoting the book, see Feldman (1989).

11. Suyuan's second husband, Canning, accompanies June to China and narrates part of Suyuan's story. In the film, June travels to China alone (which seems to contradict an earlier statement that she is not fluent in Mandarin), but Suyuan's story is still narrated briefly by Canning. To my knowledge, no critic of either the film or the novel has analyzed the effect of this lone male narrator who provides crucial information about the central story in *The Joy Luck Club*.

12. Coincidentally, Tan had already adapted "The Moon Lady" into a children's book illustrated by Gretchen Schields. She also performs the abridged audio version of her book, which excises the Ying Ying–Lena storyline entirely. (Apparently, a few scenes from this storyline were shot but did not make the final cut; see http://goldsca. com/Personalities/ Nuyenfrance/nuyenfrance.html.)

13. Avins, 1993, 2:14. According to the article, both Tan and producer Janet Yang were approached by members of a preview audience and praised for their performances in the film. This was not an isolated case; filmmaker Jessica Yu (1993b) reports that she was repeatedly mistaken for Ming-Na Wen at the 1993 Telluride Film Festival.

14. In addition to an actor's performance, mise-en-scène can also construct ethnicity. For example, Tamlyn Tomita's costume in the hairdresser's scene (a white cashmere jacket over a red silk blouse and black slacks) went a long way toward helping this particular viewer see beyond her non-Chinese features, as those colors are favored by

many Chinese American women and not by Asian American women of other ethnicities (in my experience). Of course, some aspects of the mise-en-scène may receive less attention than a lead actor's wardrobe. Charlie Chin, who portrayed "band member #5," reports that he nearly lost his mustache when "the make-up person patiently told me that Chinese men didn't wear mustaches in the 1930's" (1993, 5).

15. This discussion took place on the Internet newsgroup alt. asian-movies during the fall of 1993. I am grateful to Michael Raine for this information. Although Wang apparently insisted on casting only Mandarin speakers in the roles of Chinese women, Russell Wong (in the role of a Chinese man) is clearly dubbed. For a discussion of Chinese mistranslations in Tan's novels, see Sau-Ling Wong's "'Sugar Sisterhood'" (1995b). George Tseo (1996) also examines Tan's translations and comments on differences between the film's English subtitles and the spoken Mandarin.

16. See Ron Miller's emphasis on parallels between Polly Bemis and Rosalind Chao in . . . *Thousand Pieces of Gold*. I might also cite Chao's statement that she felt "a personal tie" to Tan's novel ("L.A. Woman" 1990), but this article can hardly be considered promotion for the film, as it was published in 1990.

17. For an account of the open casting call held in Flushing, Queens, in the fall of 1992, see C. Smith (1992).

18. Levitt and Wang are quoted saying essentially the same thing in Avins (1993); Levitt's name is misspelled Levin in that article.

19. In the finished film, the characters on the pier do not repeat this story; it is possible that Wang is misremembering an incident associated with filming the scene on the roadside. (Wang's imperfect memory is evident elsewhere in the interview, when he confuses the characters played by Christopher Rich and Andrew McCarthy.)

20. Rose's grandmother, played by Vivian Wu, is not named in the film, at least not in the English subtitles.

21. Asked point-blank "Which daughter is most like you?" Tan declines to single out any of the characters (Chatfield-Taylor 1989, 179).

22. I am indebted to Karen Gaffney, who first suggested this autobiographical interpretation as one of many possible readings of *The Joy Luck Club* in a seminar at the University of Delaware.

23. Hajari (1993) quotes France Nuyen (Ying Ying): "Joy Luck represents the fantasy of every misunderstood child. . . . You want to realize that your mother never really was mean to you. In real life that kind of communication rarely happens."

24. Taking a different psychoanalytic tack, Rey Chow argues that as the mothers *are seen*, reconciliation is forestalled. Chow's account highlights the paradox of the narratives of China: the mothers supposedly narrate what they saw, but the force of cinematic

convention overtakes their ability to describe their vision, rendering the mothers as spectacles to be seen. Chow argues that the mothers in *The Joy Luck Club* are "encrypted texts, gestural archives, and memory palaces" whose visual apprehensibility reveals "what Walter Benjamin calls the 'optical unconscious'. . . . The resulting aesthetic effect is not one of identity with but one of a distant fascination for this awesome 'animal' and 'being' which strikes us as spectacle and drama, and in front of which we lose control of our bodies—we cry" (1998, 107–8). Chow is speaking almost exclusively about scenes of the mothers in China, not of their encounters with their daughters in the United States, where they assert what it is that they see.

MARY ELLEN SNODGRASS ON THE FUNCTION OF STORYTELLING IN *THE JOY LUCK CLUB*

One of Amy Tan's most successful modes of fictional expression is the internal story. She learned to value narrative in childhood and explained in *The Opposite of Fate: A Book of Musings* (2003) that, from age seven, she listened nightly to the reading of her father, John Tan, from a bedtime storybook. She recalled, "What I loved most was listening to his voice" (p. 336). Because of prodigious reading skills and impatience, she finished the book at one sitting and went to the library for works of her own choosing. Paramount to a departure from father-read stories was her wish to pace the events of narrative to suit her own thoughts and needs for closure. The decision prefaced an adult career built on voicing human stories in complex, many-layered novels.

Of narrative-within-narrative, Tan explained at the 1998 annual American Library Association convention in Washington, D.C., that storytelling is "a deliberate derangement of the mind," a reordering of logic and exorcism of past fears to reveal pertinent insights (Eberhart). From illustrative character anecdotes and fables, she concluded that life is neither planned nor totally random. She pictured life with a womanly image—"a crazy quilt of love, pieced together, torn apart, repaired over and over again, and strong enough to protect us all" (*Ibid.*). Kitty Benedict, a reviewer for the *Hartford*

Courant, remarked that such narrative has special meaning for women in patriarchal marriages: "The way out of this bondage, imposed by man's need to subjugate and deny women their autonomy, is for the memories of mothers to be handed down honestly to their daughters" (Benedict, p. C10).

Such buoyant oral narrative is the source of *The Joy Luck Club* (1989), a mesh of fables and exempla that the author gleaned from her mother. The novel opens with the tale of a swan that used to be a duck, a fable about delayed ambitions. The story introduces the novel's psychological underpinnings of four Chinese mothers who maintain hopelessly high expectations of their Amerasian daughters. Critic Amy Ling notes that the daughters admire the mothers for their courage and ingenuity and are touched by the hardships of feudal marriage and silencing that the older generation of women encountered in China. Ling adds that, simultaneously, the Chinese-American daughters are "exasperated by their mothers' impossible demands; resentful of their mothers' intrusions on their lives, and sometimes humiliated and ashamed of their stubborn, superstitious, out-of-place Old World ways" (Ling, p. 133). Thus, storytelling becomes a paradox of autobiographical gifts, history, and admonition.

The avian tale is the introit to the first episode, in which June Woo replaces her mother Suyuan at the mah jong table after the mother's death from brain aneurysm. The substitution is a significant intergenerational moment after the first loss of a club member and the rise of the initial first-generation Chinese-American into a parent's place. Canning Woo accounts for his wife's sudden death as the result of holding ideas inside and allowing them to exceed their limits and explode. Suyuan's peers—An-mei Hsu, Lindo Jong, and Ying-ying St. Clair— regret that she died like a rabbit, a quick-legged, but small-framed mammal that ceases to exist without completing its life's business. Subsequent anecdotes and vignettes serve as a reclamation of Suyuan's individuality and a re-creation of her strengths as an aid to her less-than-successful daughter.

At a dramatic moment in club member An-mei's life, the author interposes another story, an orderly fable of magpies and a turtle. Reunited with her unnamed mother, An-mei listens to the tale of her mother's seven tears that fall into the turtle's mouth. The turtle transforms the droplets into seven pearly eggs, which yield seven magpies. The birds fly away laughing, a symbol of exploiters who turn other people's sufferings into joy. On the duo's seven-day journey to Tientsin, the mother's stories are so entrancing that An-mei forgets her sorrow at leaving Ningpo. The stories continue in Wu Tsing's house, where An-mei falls asleep in her mother's arms to the sound of her voice, a form of reassurance that relieves the child of insecurity during the move from her former home.

The novel exalts storytelling as a prop during threatening times. When An-mei's mother lies dying of an overdose of bitter poison, the turtle story returns in a dream with An-mei in the place of the turtle and the magpies above drinking the pond dry of her tears. In adulthood, she rejects psychiatrists as birds drinking the sufferers' tears. She resets her mother's story in modern times by describing the peasant revolt against coercion and the shout from rebels that causes millions of birds to fall dead. For good reason, An-mei pictures herself in the role of a hard-shelled beast that moves slowly, carefully among dangers. The image expresses a subconscious choice of position in the fable as compassionate, tear-eating turtle rather than laughing magpie.

Tan earned critical regard for her ability to relate events and reflections from distinct voices. She took one episode as the source for *The Moon Lady* (1992), her first children's story, which contains myths about the marriage of the sun and moon and about the master archer's receipt of a magic peach, which his mate steals and eats in one gulp. Tan found that such storytelling for young readers requires discipline: "A story must go in direct line from beginning to end; it cannot afford to get sidetracked by long, descriptive passages. . . . There's also more freedom. The freedom has to do with the possibilities that can happen with a children's story" (Loer, p. E4). Her assessment destroys the illusion among non-writers that composing children's literature is easy.

BELLA ADAMS ON CONFLICTING MEANINGS IN JING-MEI'S STORY

In *The Joy Luck Club*, Jing-mei contemplates the meaning of 'life's importance', a green jade pendant given to her by Suyuan, also coming up with different interpretative possibilities, none of which are final:

> What if . . . this curving line branching into three oval shapes is a pomegranate tree and that my mother was . . . wishing me fertility and posterity? What if my mother really meant the carvings were a branch of pears to give me purity and honesty? Or ten-thousand-year droplets from the magic mountain, giving me my life's direction and a thousand years of fame and immortality? (197–8)

Significantly, Jing-mei's questions go unanswered, even though she wears the pendant close to her skin like Suyuan wore it close to hers, this closeness obviously not being close enough to finalize the meaning of the pendant and by implication the Chinese mother (208). The fact that green can mean regeneration/degeneration and something/nothing, alongside Jing-mei's ideas/'no idea' (198) about the green jade pendant, reveals something not about green but about meaning, about *how* green means. . . .

Already, Jing-mei's narrative has highlighted the undesirability and impossibility of intergenerational/intercultural reconciliation and, in the process, the 'dark' side of those readings that represent *The Joy Luck Club* wholly in terms of reconciliation. Even as Suyuan's representative at the Joy Luck Club and on the trip to China, she cannot be her mother. They are two different women, a difference 'darkly' reinforced by the life/death opposition so central to the text and the mother–daughter relationships therein. But *The Joy Luck Club* cannot stop here, however, in silence, death and a situation where the (m)other is unpresentable even to her own daughter. It has to negotiate the difference between life/death, daughter/mother and one/other.

This pressure comes from the narrative itself in the sense that Suyuan's 'unfinished business' (19), the family reunion planned by her for forty years, compels Jing-mei to speak for and about the (m)other. This pressure is not only emotional and historical but also linguistic. Indeed, a fundamental assumption about language, that it has to mean, although not necessarily reliably, compels Jing-mei to represent Suyuan via proxy and portrait. This assumption is negatively articulated several times in the text, most obviously when Jing-mei's 'aunties' accord a meaning to her claim that she does not know and therefore cannot say anything about Suyuan. Whether brought about by death, not knowing and not speaking, it is impossible not to make silence meaningful. And, it is with this insight about the impossibility of stopping at the 'dark' condition of postmodernity that *The Joy Luck Club* ends. . . .

So what then does Jing-mei say in 'A Pair of Tickets' about 'Chineseness', specifically on the train journey, in the hotel shower and on meeting her sisters for the first time, and is it possible to read her comments as operating within the tradition of *jaw jieh*? To begin with the train journey: 'The minute our train leaves the Hong Kong border and enters Shenzhen, China, I feel different. . . . And I think, My mother was right. I am becoming Chinese' (267). Jing-mei's experience of becoming Chinese certainly seems to assume an essentialism based on 'returning the native to [a] natural habitat'[82] that is 'faithful to the geopolitical borders of the sovereign and colonial China, and more so to the conceptual and symbolic boundaries of East and West.' . . .

Eventually arriving at the hotel, apparently too grand for 'communist China' (276–7), Jing-mei takes a shower: 'The hotel has provided little packets of shampoo which, upon opening, I discover is the consistency and color of hoisin sauce. This is more like it, I think. This is China. And I rub some in my damp hair' (278). Arguably, this comment of Jing-mei's is essentialist in that 'Chineseness' is discoverable in a packet of shampoo. . . .

From hair roots to cultural roots: Jing-mei finally meets her Chinese sisters, a poignant moment marked by the taking of a Polaroid photograph. The photograph promotes a sense of unity not only between siblings but also between them and their dead mother: 'Together we look like our mother' (288). 'This composite image', remarks Bonnie TuSmith, 'reflects the novel's communal subtext, which works as a counterpoint to the textual surface of individualistic strife'. Reinforcing these hierarchies of surface/depth and individuality/communality, TuSmith proclaims that 'underneath the skin, we (mother/daughter, Chinese/American, etc.) are all one'.[86] This hierarchy is reinforced by Jing-mei: 'And now I also see what part of me is Chinese. It is so obvious. It is my family. It is in our blood. After all these years, it can finally be let go' (288). While 'it' generates some ambiguity, it does hark back to a comment made by Suyuan about being born Chinese and feeling/thinking Chinese: '"Someday you will see," said my mother. "It is in your blood waiting to be let go"' (267). Jing-mei's use of such powerful words as 'family' and 'blood' does seem to lend support to the argument about oneness underneath the skin or, more formally, togetherness reflected in the photograph.

However, this reflection is put into question by the last two paragraphs of *The Joy Luck Club*. Even before this, Jing-mei problematizes the privileging of the communal when on looking at her sisters' faces she 'see[s] no trace of [her] mother in them' (287). Her inability to trace her mother is quickly passed over via the reference to family and blood. Next come the photograph paragraphs: 'The flash of the Polaroid goes off and my father hands me the snapshot. My sisters and I watch quietly together, eager to see what develops'. Significantly, oneness develops in terms of a representation: 'The gray-green surface changes to the bright colors of our three images, sharpening and deepening all at once' (288). That the images *in*, or, more properly, *on* the photograph develop all at once, and that they do so *before* Jing-mei's unspoken proclamation of togetherness outside the photograph, would seem to suggest that the textual surface effects the communal subtext. TuSmith's hierarchy is thus reversed: an analogy on the textual surface unites image and referent, and, crucially, it is this apparent unity that effects, rather than reflects, Jing-mei's sense of togetherness. . . .

114

Jing-mei . . . represents her identity, her family and China in terms of an essential 'Chineseness'. Clearly, then, the notion of ethnic essence circulates in the text, and it is to this apparently unproblematic formulation of 'Chineseness' that Tan's more critical commentators direct their critiques. But what is also clear is the fact that Jing-mei's representation of self and others has its basis in a photograph. Similarly, becoming Chinese and discovering China depend on a myth, a guidebook and a shampoo. This emphasis on the cultural underpinnings of 'Chineseness' and *how* Jing-mei says what she says suggests a critical, if not a strategic negotiation of essentialism. By moving from 'blood' to a photograph and, more crucially, by focusing on the photograph's formal dimension—'the gray-green surface', the bright colors' and 'three images sharpening and deepening all at once'—questions emerge about the nature of Jing-mei's 'bloody' epiphany. If 'Chineseness' is 'so obvious[ly] . . . in [Jing-mei's] blood' (288), why refer to a photograph at all? Indeed, what *kind* of ethnic essence depends on a myth, a guidebook, a shampoo and a photograph to make it obvious?

* * *

It is with this less than 'bloody' ending that this chapter ends, although not in some 'sweet' or fairy-tale way. From the opening vignette and the Kweilin story to the final chapter, *The Joy Luck Club* focuses on change, movement and difference. Crucially, its different parts, functioning synecdochically, not symbolically, resist reconciliation and other terms endorsing closure, wholeness and oneness. Difference proves fundamental to *The Joy Luck Club*; indeed, without it neither dialogues nor relationships/identities would be possible. Rather than envisaging difference wholly in negative terms, as that which generates upset, irritation and silence between the two generations of women, can it not also be understood more positively, especially given that a final reconciliation is both undesirable and impossible? For Jing-mei, it implies death and, less dramatically, as is the case for the other daughters, a loss of self. Hence reconciliation is understood in terms of fighting tigers and women armed with kitchen utensils and knitting needles (252, 183–4), preserving difference between Chinese mothers and American-born daughters to their mutual benefit.

Notes
82. Chow, 'Violence', 92.
86. TuSmith, *All My Relatives*, 68.

MAGALI CORNIER MICHAEL ON AN ALTERNATIVE VIEW OF THE NOVEL'S CONCLUSION

When Jing-mei finally meets her twin sisters, she is initially startled that they do not look like their mother. However, she notes in them something familiar, which triggers a recognition of the part of her that is Chinese: "It is so obvious. It is my family" (331). When minutes later she examines the Polaroid picture her father takes of her with the twins, Jing-mei notes that "together we look like our mother" (332). Although many scholars have criticized the ending of *The Joy Luck Club* for depending on what David Li calls a kind of "chromosomal trope of cultural reproduction,"[76] I would argue that Tan's novel as a whole presents a more complex picture of cultural reproduction that places emphasis on the family over and above genetics. Indeed, the entire novel stresses not only the role of the family in cultural production and reproduction but also the dynamic possibilities of conceptions of the extended family with ties based on friendship, empathy, and care. Jing-mei's recognition that her family—and not just her mother—represents the part of her that is Chinese indicates a more inclusive notion of family that pushes beyond mere genealogy despite her subsequent reference to blood ties. What connects Jing-mei to her half sisters is not just a common genetic pool but, more crucially, their shared pain of having lost a loving mother. Furthermore, they share their mother's Chinese-inflected valuing of family, which she put into practice as she raised her Chinese American family in the United States and, simultaneously, continued to search via letters for her twin daughters in China. That their resemblance to their mother occurs only when they appear together on the Polaroid is a function not so much of genetics but rather of their meeting's representing Suyuan's dream of bringing together the children of her two different marriages and lives in different geographical spaces and cultural traditions. For Jing-mei, meeting her half sisters provides her with a closer connection not only to her mother, about whose past life and pains she knew so little, but also to her Chinese cultural heritage.[77] Having flown halfway around the globe to China, Jing-mei locates the part of her that is Chinese in her family; but, as the novel makes clear throughout its pages, her family includes not only her immediate nuclear family but also an extended family: her two half sisters in China and the members of the Joy Luck Club at home in San Francisco. Moreover, her extended family connects her to the part of her that is Chinese precisely because it is the site of the production and reproduction of ever-evolving Chinese cultural traditions.

Tan's novel depicts all four mothers and daughters as actively negotiating their identities as Chinese Americans in order to assert themselves as subjects with agency, albeit in different ways and to differing extents. Although part of that process of negotiation occurs on the level of mother–daughter relationships, what ultimately reconnects the mothers and daughters are not their genetic ties but rather certain parallel experiences as women marked by their Chinese heritage—particularly experiences of patriarchal oppression within familial relationships, racially marked oppression within American culture, and the difficult negotiation of a Chinese American identity.[78] Moreover, the parallels between the four mother–daughter relationships and the existence of the Joy Luck Club as a community that encompasses and at times helps to negotiate these relationships highlights an interdependence that extends beyond the mother–daughter relationships. *The Joy Luck Club* thus participates in what Chu describes as a tendency within Asian American writing to invent "a subject who combines independence, mobility and outspokenness with a deep sense of affinity with familial and communal others."[79]

The novel's positioning of the four mother–daughter relationships within the larger context of the Joy Luck Club community not only shifts attention away from an exclusive focus on the mother–daughter dyads but also offers a larger, more dynamic familial structure that does not depend solely on genealogy and thus offers the flexibility that Chinese immigrants and their descendants require if they are to create communities to sustain their Chinese heritage while living in the United States and within the context of American culture.[80] For example, Jing-mei's reconnection with her mother through her meeting of her twin half sisters and with her Chinese heritage through both her physical trip to China and her understanding of the function of her family as a bridge to her Chinese heritage occurs as a consequence of the existence of the Joy Luck Club. Without the caring, interdependent relationships that the Joy Luck Club provides for the mothers, Suyuan's search for her daughters would most likely have died with her own physical death. Not only do the Joy Luck Club aunties know of Suyuan's relentless quest—which she had not shared with either her husband or daughter—but they organize the meeting between Jing-mei and her twin half sisters by writing to the twins in Chinese (something Jing-mei cannot do) and raising the money necessary to send Jing-mei to China. The aunties' assertion as Suyuan's friends-sisters and their collective agency in making Suyuan's wish come true, as well as Jing-mei's assertion of self and of individual agency in undertaking the trip to China, thus both depend on the Joy Luck Club as a collective entity with collective agency that makes possible individual agency. As Chu notes, *The Joy Luck Club* is "a novel whose multiple narratives construct both mothers and daughters as Asian [more specifically, Chinese] American subjects";[81] but I want to add that this construction occurs crucially within the context of a dynamic, extended family-community.

Through its depiction of the Joy Luck Club, Amy Tan's novel offers a useful model for reimagining agency at the turn of the twenty-first century within the context of the United States as an immigrant nation that is growing increasingly multicultural. This multicultural aspect of the United States creates not only tensions but also the possibility of coalition building to deal with those tensions and of creating new frameworks out of the various traditions brought to this country in order to negotiate an ever-changing contemporary culture.[82] The Joy Luck Club borrows the Chinese valuing of the family and its relationships of interdependence but alters traditional Confucian notions of the family to get rid of the hierarchies of power and dependence on patrilineage that structure them. Through a more symmetrical distribution of power, the Joy Luck Club retains different roles for its various members while simultaneously rejecting a hierarchical structure. For example, although the mothers cook the meals for the club gatherings and play mah jong while their husbands play cards after the meal, the mothers share with their husbands an equal, democratic voice and vote in Joy Luck Club decisions. Moreover, the club values but does not privilege blood ties; indeed, the novel depicts a number of connecting threads between the various members of the Joy Luck Club, with the primary ones being a function of their positions as first- or second-generation Chinese immigrants to the United States. Positionality and affect rather than blood ties prove to be the real glue between Joy Luck Club members, even between mothers and daughters. Moreover, the characters' sense of hope, derived from a blend of the Chinese notion of fate and the American dream, both of which contain and celebrate a participatory element, provides the impetus for their developments as agents within the context of the collective.

Although some critics have objected to the novel's ending as overly utopian, I see this utopian ending as serving the vital function of consolidating its hopeful evocation of an alternative form of familial community as necessary both for the characters' survival and for their assertion of agency. Indeed, the novel offers an alternative model of kinship based on affinities deriving from specific cultural positioning, which creates a familial community that values caring interdependence as politically efficacious in that it makes possible the negotiation of collective identity and agency and in turn of individual identity and agency within the context of the collectivity. Tan's novel thus offers a vision of Chinese American women characters who are contributing to what Ho calls "an American culture-in-the-making"[83] through their active construction of alternative, hybrid forms of identity and agency that emphasize the interconnectedness of the individual and the collective.

Notes

76. Li, *Imagining the Nation*, p. 124.

77. Heung argues that Jing-mei's reunion with her sisters performs a "melding of cross-cultural linkages" ("Daughter-Text/Mother-Text," p. 610).

78. Bow argues that Tan's novel "locates the mother/daughter relationship as the site for a reenvisioning of self both based on and potentially transcending a maternal legacy" (*Betrayal and Other Acts of Subversion*, p. 71). My argument focuses on the Joy Luck Club as encompassing the mother–daughter relationships and thus as the site for such a reenvisioning of self and of agency.

79. Chu, *Assimilating Asians*, p. 18.

80. As Heung similarly notes, "Mutual nurturance does not arise from biological or generational connections alone; rather, it is an act affirming consciously chosen allegiances" ("Daughter-Text/Mother-Text," p. 613).

81. Chu, *Assimilating Asians*, p. 22.

82. Matsuda notes that "our [Asian American] coalition does not originate in Asia. It is American" (*Where Is Your Body?* p. 173).

83. Ho, *In Her Mother's House*, p. 39.

JANE ELLIOTT ON THE STRUGGLE BETWEEN THE PAST AND THE FUTURE

In *The Joy Luck Club*, the temporal disparity between prefeminist mother and postfeminist daughter is underlined by the novel's immigration narratives, which associate the mothers with a premodern China and the daughters with an ultramodern America, as if they had not one but several generations between them.[13] In so doing, the novel suggests that immigration to America is the only choice for Chinese women who desire their female children to be free, and it refuses to consider America's role in creating the very oppression the novel associates with China. As one of the mothers recounts, "My mother, she suffered. . . . There is nothing more to understand. That was China. That was what people did back then. They had no choice."[14] In contrast, America is presented as a land of openness and possibility, particularly for women: "[O]ver there [in America] nobody will say [my daughter's] worth is measured by the loudness of her husband's belch. . . . And over there she will always be too full to swallow any sorrow!" (Tan 17). Such passages obviously enact the sort of privileging of Western modernity as both inevitable and always an improvement for women that transnational and postcolonial feminist theorists have frequently criticized. As Sau-Ling Cynthia Wong puts it, "[F]or the feminist audience, the Chinese American mother/daughter dyad in *The Joy Luck Club* . . . allegorizes a Third World/First World encounter that allows mainstream American feminism to construct itself in a flattering, because depoliticized, manner."[15] Because she possesses the purported advantages of mainstream American feminism, the daughter's choices serve as a means of representing the tension between earlier, supposedly Chinese premodern womanhood and the assimilated Western femininity America offers. . . .

Despite major differences . . . among the various mother/daughter pairs in *The Joy Luck Club*, the past, in the form of the mother, overwhelms the future, in the form of the daughter, in every case. Most obviously, this eradication of the future happens in *The Joy Luck Club* owing to an overload of mother/daughter sympathy that thwarts the usual powers of sentimental emotion. As I have already suggested, the overidentification of women with their mothers became a given in the late 1970s and 1980s American cultural landscape. . . .

In *The Joy Luck Club*, such fusion through shared pain characterizes many of the mother/daughter relationships, particularly those located in China. In the story that mother An-Mei tells about her relationship with her own mother, for example, this pain is the defining element in their relationship. Although she has spent much of her childhood without her mother, An-Mei recognizes her immediately when they meet, recounting, "I knew she was my mother, because I could feel her pain" (Tan 216). An-Mei's mother attempts to caution her daughter against showing too much of this pain, as others might use it to their own advantage:

> "Now you see . . . why it is useless to cry. Your tears do not wash away your sorrows. They feed someone else's joy. And that is why you must learn to swallow your own tears."
>
> But after my mother finished her story, I looked at her and saw she was crying. And I also began to cry again, that this was our fate, to live like two turtles seeing the watery world together from the bottom of the little pond. (Tan 217)

Echoing the images of liquidity associated with both mother/daughter merging and sentimental fusion, this passage represents mother and daughter as almost swimming in tears. And, while An-Mei's mother suggests that An-Mei's tears may benefit someone else, that dynamic doesn't define the mother/daughter relationship. Rather, the tears of one merely prompt the tears of the other, locking them in an endless cycle of mutually consuming grief that threatens to drown them both. If daughters represent the abstract future and mothers the painful and particular past, mother/daughter fusion in suffering figures an overload of past pain such that the abstract, painless future is eradicated entirely. To put it another way, mother/daughter fusion works so well that the daughter's identification with the mother's pain eradicates her own access to futurity. . . .

Given that the daughter's lack of futurity arises here from the mother's suffering and lack of power, the more general solution would seem to be for the mother to have power so that, when the daughter identifies with her, the daughter incorporates her mother's strength rather than her oppression and misery. In fact, *The Joy Luck Club* suggests that the opposite is true: as we learn from Lindo and Waverly's story cycle, strong mothers produce miserable daughters as well. Even as a young girl, mother Lindo seems able to manipulate the oppressive systems around her in China by using the very rules that confine her to produce the effects she desires. This power persists even in America, where Lindo has the most obviously successful daughter, the onetime chess prodigy Waverly. At first, it appears that Lindo is able to pass on her talents to Waverly, whose aptitude for chess resembles her mother's ability to manipulate systems to her own benefit. Although Waverly is pleased with her chess triumphs, she becomes increasingly frustrated with Lindo's tendency to want to claim credit for those victories, and the two have a fight. Waverly loses this battle, and afterward she never plays chess so successfully or confidently again. This series of events suggests that Waverly can have power only as long as she remains tied to and aligned with her mother; for Waverly, though, this power doesn't seem her own precisely because she remains under her mother's control. To put it another way, Lindo cannot help Waverly learn to manipulate the system because, for Waverly, Lindo is the system. Waverly's story suggests that, because the mother's power is experienced by the daughter as a threatening force, the mother cannot transmit whatever power she possesses to her daughter: instead, in keeping with the zero-sum dynamic, the mother's power immediately becomes power over rather than power shared by the daughter. In a fashion that perfectly metaphorizes the mutually exclusive vectors of past and future, the mother's strength cannot be shared with the daughter but rather works against her, such that the past still triumphs over the future.

In every case, it seems, the past, in the form of the mother, overwhelms the future, in the form of the daughter. This sense of almost uncanny uniformity in the mother/daughter relationship is underscored in *The Joy Luck Club* by what Shirley Lim calls the mother's position as "the figure not only of maternality but also of racial consciousness."[25] The novel repeatedly associates its vision of this racial consciousness with nonrational or magical models of cause and effect.[26] One of the sections in the novel begins with a sort of parable that encapsulates the power this nonrational causality has in the novel: a mother tells her daughter not to ride her bike around the corner because a Chinese book called *The Twenty-Six Malignant Gates* says that bad things will happen to the daughter away from her house. The daughter becomes frustrated when the mother refuses to explain what these bad things are and finally begins to yell: "'*You can't tell me because you don't know! You don't know anything!' And the girl ran outside, jumped on her bicycle, and in her hurry to get away, she fell before she even reached the corner*" (Tan 87, emphasis in original). Thus, the mysterious knowledge associated with the Chinese book trumps the daughter's supposed agency, turning even her defiance into a means of fulfilling its prophecy: whatever action the daughter takes still ends in reinforcing both the mysterious forces of Chinese causality and the infallibility of the mother. That the mother and daughter are unnamed suggests the way that this vignette serves as a kind of ur-narrative that underlies all the mother/daughter relationships in *The Joy Luck Club*. Behind the rational American version of cause and effect, the novel insists, a more mysterious set of forces is at work, bending any action to fit a predetermined outcome. Because this form of inexorable determination is associated with both the mother and a racial consciousness associated with the mother country, so to speak, it serves as a kind of metaphor for the power of the past: the inexorable weight of the past determines events much the way the mysterious, magical powers of a supposedly premodern Chinese causality do, molding what could have been different futures into the preformed image of the past.

The Joy Luck Club thematizes this sense of overdetermination through its proliferation of mother/daughter pairs. As Dana Heller points out, "Balance is structurally foregrounded [by the novel] in symmetrical pairings, a reiteration of fours. There are four mothers, four daughters, four directions, and four corners of the mah-jongg table."[27] Among the four mother/daughter pairs, we also find a balanced set of oppositions: the novel depicts a mother who is a victim of the system of Chinese causality (Ying-Ying), a mother who is a victim of the American system of causality (An-Mei), a mother who is powerful in her manipulation of Chinese causality (Lindo), and a mother who is powerful in her belief in American causality (Suyuan). Yet this balanced set of opposing situations collapses into a single disastrous result: all the daughters feel powerless and stuck, unable to embrace the positive futurity that the novel implies is theirs by right of having been born in the right place and time. As An-Mei puts it,

> I was raised the Chinese way; I was taught to desire nothing, to swallow other people's misery, to eat my own bitterness. . . .
> And even though I taught my daughter the opposite, still she came out the same way! Maybe it is because she was born to me and she was born a girl. And I was born to my mother and I was born a girl. All of us are like stairs, one step after another, going up and down, but all going the same way. (Tan 215)

Using language reminiscent of *The Women's Room*'s description of a weaving in which all the strands are the same color, *The Joy Luck Club* suggests the way in which the mother/daughter relationship figures the link between totalization and static time: because the mother and daughter are invariably the same, the difference that should inevitably arise with the passage of time is erased, so that the same world is reproduced in the same way, ad infinitum. Ultimately, then, the resonance of the mother/daughter relationship arises not only from the way in which it consistently demonstrates the power of the past but also from the way in which it suggests the overdetermination of that process, the way in which every possible permutation of the mother/daughter equation returns the same bleak answer. The mother/daughter relationship is thus a kind of engine of totalization: from its disparate dysfunctional relationships, it produces the same identical effect—a daughter who is no freer than her mother before her.

Notes
13. Much of the literary criticism written about *The Joy Luck Club* focuses on mother/daughter dynamics. See, for example, Braendlin, "Mother/Daughter Dialog(ic)s"; Heung, "Daughter-Text/

Mother-Text"; Mountain, "'The Struggle of Memory'"; Shear, "Generational Differences"; and Wong, "'Sugar Sisterhood.'"

14. Tan, *The Joy Luck Club*, 241. Hereafter cited in text as Tan.

15. Wong, "'Sugar Sisterhood,'" 181.

25. Lim, "Japanese-American Women's Life Stories," 293, quoted in Heung, "Daughter-Text/Mother-Text," 28.

26. Examples of this nonrational causality in the novel include the omnipotence of thoughts, the inexorability of predetermined fate, and the ability of the seemingly extraneous to create material effects—for example, through the doctrine of feng shui. On feng shui in *The Joy Luck Club*, see Hamilton, "*Feng Shui*." For another discussion of fate, determination, and its connection to Chinese experience in the novel, see Shear, "Generational Differences."

27. Heller, *Family Plots*, 121–22.

Works by Amy Tan

The Joy Luck Club, 1989.

"The Language of Discretion" and "Mother Tongue" (critical essays), 1990.

The Kitchen God's Wife, 1991.

The Moon Lady (children's book), 1992.

The Chinese Siamese Cat (children's book), 1994.

The Hundred Secret Senses, 1995.

The Year of No Flood, 1995.

The Bonesetter's Daughter, 2001.

The Opposite of Fate: A Book of Musings (nonfiction), 2003.

Saving Fish from Drowning, 2005.

Annotated Bibliography

Adams, Bella. *Amy Tan*. Manchester, United Kingdom: Manchester University Press, 2005.

This recent book-length study of Amy Tan's work is comprehensive and substantial. Each of her major novels (before 2005)—*The Joy Luck Club, The Kitchen God's Wife, The Hundred Secret Senses,* and *The Bonesetter's Daughter*—is discussed in a separate, in-depth chapter. As scholars reflect on the author's phenomenal success following her first novel, they isolate some critical and controversial issues that are still being debated. Adams deals with the issues pertaining to Tan's representation of identities, the authenticity of her details, and the "commercial" exploitation of "the exotic," such as Asian or non-American individuals. The author is assuming that her readers will have a substantial background in the related fields of study, such as multiculturalism and feminist perspectives in literature.

Brown, Anne E., and Marjanne El Gooz, eds. *International Women's Writing: New Landscapes of Identity*. Westport, Conn.: Greenwood Press, 1995.

This volume is part of the series Contributions in Women's Studies. The work focuses on the concept of identity from a crosscultural and, specifically, feminist perspective. Each of the 23 collected essays expands on the assumption that no fixed or permanent definition of "identity" exists. "Identity" is looked at in different racial, political, economic, and cultural contexts. In addition to the chapter on Amy Tan, there is commentary on such diverse artists as Jean Rhys, Bharati Mukherjee, Nadine Gordimer, Dacia Maraini, Medbh McGuckian, and Isabel Allende.

Brown-Guillory, Elizabeth, ed. *Women of Color: Mother-Daughter Relationships in 20th-Century Literature*. Austin: University of Texas Press, 1996.

This volume collects essays on the topic of mother/daughter relationships among the titular "women of color" that were presented at the South Central Modern Language Association conference in 1996. Attention is focused on the observation that daughters must "see" their mothers objectively, must reach some level of understanding of their own mothers before they can achieve any sustainable sense of identity. In contrast, mothers see reflections of themselves when looking at their daughters and may be reminded of their early aspirations, illusions, and mistakes. This mutual need makes the mother/daughter relationship particularly complex and dynamic. A chapter on the mother/daughter pairs in *The Joy Luck Club* is insightful.

Chu, Patricia P. *Assimilating Asians: Gendered Strategies of Authorship in Asian America*. Durham, N.C., and London: Duke University Press, 2000.

This study of Asian-American life and culture presents and discusses the scholarship on the phenomenal popularity in the West of recently published novels by Asian-American writers. Questions are raised about the authenticity of representation, the stereotypical assumptions about the significant majority of Asians who do not become American immigrants or even wish to, and the institutional resistance of American-born citizens to regard Asian Americans as authentic American citizens. Students already knowledgeable about these issues will benefit from Chu's findings. The author devotes a long chapter to *The Joy Luck Club*.

Elliott, Jane. *Popular Feminist Fiction as American Allegory: Representing National Time*. New York: Palgrave Macmillan, 2008.

Jane Elliott is credited with formulating an original approach to the feminist study of literature and the study of feminist literature. Her book builds on the assumptions and perspectives established during the now decades-long period of feminist engagement in cultural and political issues. The depth and sophistication of the author's multilayered research make for a nuanced analysis. Her discussion of *The Joy Luck Club* includes important insights for any student of the novel.

Feng, Peter X. *Identities in Motion: Asian American Film and Video.* Durham, N.C., and London, Duke University Press, 2002.

This volume documents both the challenge of bringing a vast and turbulent history to the screen and, more complexly, the way in which both film and history reflect and record reality without—themselves—being reality. In his introduction, the author acknowledges the paradoxical nature of his title— "Identities in Motion"—because identity is generally understood to be a relatively fixed concept arrived at after reflection and analysis and because the word has a different meaning when followed by "pictures" (identity in motion pictures). Feng's study includes discussions of both mainstream and marginal films and many photos of scenes illustrating his points. The author also discusses critics' reviews including Richard Ebert's factually incorrect review of the 1988 film *A Thousand Pieces of Gold*. Other films discussed include *The Wedding Banquet* (1993) and *The Joy Luck Club* (1993).

Ho, Wendy. *In Her Mother's House: The Politics of Asian American Mother-Daughter Writing.* Walnut Creek, Calif.: Alta Mira Press, Rowman & Littlefield, 1999.

Drawing on the fictional writings of Amy Tan, Maxine Hong Kingston, and Fae Myenne Ng, Wendy Ho assembles a portrait of the mother/daughter and other familial relationships that extend beyond the familiar categories of literary, feminist, and gender perspectives. Her wide-ranging discussions are centered on the distinctive and recurring content of the talk stories told by Asian-American women to their American-born daughters to convey warnings, secrets, advice, and privileged information about the mother's experiences in an oppressive patriarchal society.

Huntley, E.D. *Amy Tan: A Critical Companion.* Westport, Conn., and London: Greenwood Press, 1998.

This companion book for reading Tan covers her first three novels with a lengthy chapter devoted to each and a biographical sketch that pays special attention to what influences led the author to the writer's life. Another chapter addresses her role in the relatively recent emergence of Asian-American female writers and the widespread popularity of their novels. A bibliography for Tan's work in general and for each of her novels in particular concludes this accessible and highly readable introduction to the author.

Lee, Mabel, and Meng Hua, eds. *Cultural Dialogue and Misreading*. New South Wales, Australia: Wild Peony Pty. Ltd. & Contributors, 1997.

This substantial volume (more than 400 pages) is a selection of papers presented at the International Conference on Cultural Dialogue and Cultural Misreading held in Beijing in October 1995. The participating scholars share an enthusiastic interest in the richness and diversity of the world's literatures. Topics addressed include cultural relativism, political writing, Eurocentrism, translation and misreading, cultural identity formation in multicultural contexts, and the limits and uses of multiculturalism. The sophisticated content of most of these papers makes this volume most appropriate for advanced students in multicultural studies.

Ling, Amy. *Between Worlds: Women Writers of Chinese Ancestry*. Elmsford, N.Y.: Pergamon Press, 1990.

Chinese-born Amy Ling began her study of crosscultural and ethnic literature after completing her formal education. This volume is the product of her extensive effort to identify members of the title group and to locate their often out-of-print books. She is among the first to have made this effort and to have succeeded in assessing what these novels, memoirs, and stories collectively mean for and contribute to contemporary culture. Ling's last chapter, "Righting Wrongs by Writing Wrongs," is a literary goal shared by many of these writers, including Amy Tan. Collectively, these Asian-American writers know they are writing valuable history that might otherwise remain distorted or forever buried.

Michael, Magali Cornier. *New Visions of Community in Contemporary American Fiction: Tan, Kingsolver, Castillo, Morrison*. Iowa City: University of Iowa Press, 2006.

This work connects politics, literature, and the contemporary cultural phenomenon of large-scale migrations and boundary crossings, some voluntary and peaceful and some coerced and violent. The result all over the world is an unprecedented mixing of cultures and traditions around the world and the productive or destructive effects of these population shifts and newly formed multiethnic communities. The author looks at the work of four American women writers and examines their diverse ideas for reimagining what community building may look like in the twenty-first century. Amy Tan is one of the four key authors examined, and *The Joy Luck Club* is her novel most extensively discussed.

Palumbo-Liu, David, ed. *The Ethnic Canon: Histories, Institutions, and Interventions.* Minneapolis: University Press of Minnesota, 1995.

This book—most suitable for readers advanced in literary and cultural studies—addresses the complex issue of ethnic literatures as they are accepted, interwoven, and understood against and within the standards and assumptions of the prevailing canon. The distinct but sometimes overlapping meanings of "multiculturalism," "diversity," and "ethnicity" are discussed along with the history of what political and historical elements influence interpretation and selection. Controversial and contradictory readings of specific texts are also provided.

Singh, Amritjit, Joseph T. Skerrett, Jr., Robert E. Hagan, eds. *Memory, Narrative, and Identity: New Essays in Ethnic American Literature.* Boston: Northeastern University Press, 1994.

This volume of 14 collected essays is essential reading for students of American ethnic literatures. As one of the central features of ethnic literatures, memory can be put to multiple and diverse applications and purposes, from collective memory and public and institutionalized memory to the clash between competing versions of the same event, such as marginalized peoples and the "official" story that excludes them. The essay on *The Joy Luck Club* carefully examines the mothers' memories and the ways these recounted narratives influence their daughters' efforts to formulate their own identities.

Snodgrass, Mary Ellen. *Amy Tan: A Literary Companion.* Jefferson, N.C., and London: McFarland & Company, 2004.

This excellent introduction and companion to the novels of Amy Tan is well suited for both beginning and more advanced readers. The chronology of the author's life is several pages long, augmented by considerable detail about Tan's life and the author's commentary on the significance of certain influences and events. A lengthy glossary of terms of particular importance to understanding Tan's work—such as talk story, diaspora, morality tale, fate and fortune, and mah jong—is provided as well as brief discussions of each of four novels (*Saving Fish from Drowning* had not been published by the time this work was released) and genealogies for all of Tan's characters and members of her own family. The book concludes with a glossary of Chinese terms, suggested topics for writing and study projects, and a lengthy bibliography.

Contributors

Harold Bloom is Sterling Professor of the Humanities at Yale University. He is the author of 30 books, including *Shelley's Mythmaking*, *The Visionary Company*, *Blake's Apocalypse*, *Yeats*, *A Map of Misreading*, *Kabbalah and Criticism*, *Agon: Toward a Theory of Revisionism*, *The American Religion*, *The Western Canon*, and *Omens of Millennium: The Gnosis of Angels, Dreams, and Resurrection*. *The Anxiety of Influence* sets forth Professor Bloom's provocative theory of the literary relationships between the great writers and their predecessors. His most recent books include *Shakespeare: The Invention of the Human*, a 1998 National Book Award finalist, *How to Read and Why*, *Genius: A Mosaic of One Hundred Exemplary Creative Minds*, *Hamlet: Poem Unlimited*, *Where Shall Wisdom Be Found?*, and *Jesus and Yahweh: The Names Divine*. In 1999, Professor Bloom received the prestigious American Academy of Arts and Letters Gold Medal for Criticism. He has also received the International Prize of Catalonia, the Alfonso Reyes Prize of Mexico, and the Hans Christian Andersen Bicentennial Prize of Denmark.

Ben Xu teaches English at St. Mary's College in California. In 1992, he published *Situational Tensions of Critical Intellectuals: Thinking Through Literary Politics with Edward W. Said and Frank Lentriccia*.

Gloria Shen teaches in the department of comparative literature at the University of Georgia. In addition to her work on Amy Tan, Shen has written on crosscultural issues as related to race and gender, society and literature, and women's literature.

M. Marie Booth Foster teaches in the languages and literature department at Florida A&M University.

Steven P. Sondrup teaches in the department of humanities, classics, and comparative literature at Brigham Young University.

Patricia L. Hamilton teaches in the English department at Union University in Jackson, Tennessee.

Wendy Ho is a professor of Asian-American studies and women's and gender studies at the University of California at Davis. In 2001, she wrote the essay "Thinking Globally to Enrich Student Lives."

Patricia P. Chu is a professor in the department of English at George Washington University.

Peter X. Feng teaches English and women's studies at the University of Delaware.

Mary Ellen Snodgrass writes for the McFarland Literary Companions series. Her other works have profiled the writings of Barbara Kingsolver (2004) and August Wilson (2004). In 1999, she co-authored with Gary Carey *A Multicultural Dictionary of Literary Terms*.

Bella Adams is sessional lecturer in English Studies at Liverpool John Moores University.

Magali Cornier Michael, who teaches in the English department at Duquesne University, is also the author of *Feminism and the Postmodern Impulse: Post–World War II Fiction* (1996).

Jane Elliott is lecturer in the department of English and related literature at the University of York. Two earlier publications include "The Currency of Feminist Theory" (*PMLA* 121, no. 5, October 2006) and "Time of Death: The End of the 1960s and the Problem of Feminist Futurity in *The Women's Room* and *Vida*" (*Modern Fiction Studies* 52 no. 1, Spring 2006).

Acknowledgments

Ben Xu, "Memory and the Ethnic Self: Reading Amy Tan's *The Joy Luck Club*." From *Memory, Narrative, and Identity: New Essays in Ethnic American Literature*, pp. 264–68. © 1994 by Northeastern University Press and University Press of New England, Hanover, NH. Reprinted with permission.

Gloria Shen, "Born of a Stranger: Mother-Daughter Relationships and Storytelling in Amy Tan's *The Joy Luck Club*." From *International Women's Writing: New Landscapes of Identity*, pp. 233–37, 241–42. Copyright © 1995 by Anne E. Brown and Marjanne E. Goozé. Reproduced with permission of Greenwood Publishing Group, Inc., Westport, CT.

M. Marie Booth Foster, "Voice, Mind, Self: Mother-Daughter Relationships in Amy Tan's *The Joy Luck Club* and *The Kitchen God's Wife*." From *Women of Color: Mother-Daughter Relationships in 20th-Century Literature*, edited by Elizabeth Brown-Guillory, pp. 208–09, 211, 214–17, 221–22, 225. Copyright © 1996. By permission of the University of Texas Press.

Steven P. Sondrup, "Hanyu at the Joy Luck Club." From *Cultural Dialogue and Misreading*, edited by Mabel Lee and Meng Hua, pp. 400–07. © 1997 Wild Peony Pty Ltd and the individual contributors.

Patricia L. Hamilton, "Feng Shui, Astrology, and the Five Elements: Traditional Chinese Belief in Amy Tan's *The Joy Luck Club*." From *MELUS*, vol. 24, no. 2, Religion, Myth, and Ritual (Summer 1999): 125–27, 136–41, 144–45.

Wendy Ho, "Losing Your Innocence but Not Your Hope: Amy Tan's Joy Luck Mothers and Coca-Cola Daughters." From *In Her Mother's House: The Politics of Asian American Mother-Daughter Writing*, pp. 143–93. Copyright © 1999 by AltaMira Press.

Every effort has been made to contact the owners of copyrighted material and secure copyright permission. Articles appearing in this volume generally appear much as they did in their original publication with few or no editorial changes. In some cases, foreign language text has been removed from the original essay. Those interested in locating the original source will find the information cited above.

Index

·